Violence: A Very Short Introduction

VERY SHORT INTRODUCTIONS are for anyone wanting a stimulating and accessible way into a new subject. They are written by experts, and have been translated into more than 45 different languages.

The series began in 1995, and now covers a wide variety of topics in every discipline. The VSI library currently contains over 700 volumes—a Very Short Introduction to everything from Psychology and Philosophy of Science to American History and Relativity—and continues to grow in every subject area.

## Very Short Introductions available now:

## Available soon:

For more information visit our website

www.oup.com/vsi/

Philip Dwyer

# VIOLENCE

## A Very Short Introduction

# OXFORD

UNIVERSITY PRESS

Great Clarendon Street, Oxford, OX2 6DP,
United Kingdom

Oxford University Press is a department of the University of Oxford.
It furthers the University's objective of excellence in research, scholarship,
and education by publishing worldwide. Oxford is a registered trade mark of
Oxford University Press in the UK and in certain other countries

© Philip Dwyer 2022

The moral rights of the author have been asserted

First edition published in 2022

Impression: 1

Published in the United States of America by Oxford University Press
198 Madison Avenue, New York, NY 10016, United States of America

British Library Cataloguing in Publication Data
Data available

Library of Congress Control Number: 2021949067

ISBN 978-0-19-883173-0

Printed in Great Britain by
Ashford Colour Press Ltd, Gosport, Hampshire

# Contents

# Acknowledgements

I am grateful to Mark Edele, Peter Hempenstall, Michael Ondaatje, and Elizabeth Roberts-Pedersen for their enormously helpful comments and suggestions on a draft of this book, as well as to the anonymous readers. Their generous and collegial support has improved this work no end. A huge thank you to my wife Andrea, who read and corrected the manuscript. Thanks to Jordan Beavis for the Liddell Hart quote. My thanks to Andrea Keegan, Jenny Nugee, Luciana O'Flaherty, and Henry Clarke at Oxford University Press for guiding this *Very Short Introduction* to completion. Thanks too to the copy-editors, Edwin and Jackie Pritchard, for their help in bringing this book in line with the series. Brief sections in the first chapter on theorizing violence, in Chapter 2 on homicide, and in Chapter 6 on colonial violence have been adapted from earlier publications by the author, which appear in the references and the Further Reading section at the end of the book.

I was very fortunate to be a Senior Fulbright scholar at the University of Illinois, Urbana-Champaign, in the second half of 2019, where I received a very warm welcome and where I was able to write and try out some of the ideas found here. My thanks to Mark Micale for facilitating contacts there. I was also privileged to be a Visiting Fellow at All Souls College, Oxford, during Hilary Term 2020, where I was able to take more time off teaching to reflect on and write about violence. The structure of this book follows in large part an undergraduate course that I have been teaching for several years, during which the students have often challenged me to clarify my thoughts and obliged me to make connections between forms of violence that were not always self-evident. The course and the students have allowed me to delve into the nature of violence in ways that I would not have been able to otherwise. I hope they found it as rewarding as I did.

# List of illustrations

# Chapter 1
# Violence past and present

## Thinking about violence

Violence is a word that encompasses many different acts of aggression: the parent who beats his or her child, the partner who beats or kills their spouse, the mobster who eliminates a rival, the gang of young men who rape a woman, the military or the police who torture a suspect, the child soldier who is ordered to kill, the suicide terrorist who kills himself and others, the rioter who sets fire to a car, the villager who hacks his neighbour to death with a machete. The list of what constitutes violence is endless and is so pervasive across so many societies and cultures that it forces us to ask, is it part of human nature? All societies are violent, and all individuals have the capacity for violence, but not all societies and individuals are equally violent. But if violence is a constant throughout history, what does that say about us as a species? Does violence come naturally to people or do people have to overcome their reluctance to engage in violent acts? Might modern humans find it more difficult to overcome that reluctance than people in past centuries (depending on the culture in question)? Or is violence a social tool or function that is culturally dependent?

This short introduction examines violence in history in the modern world, from the mid-18th century onwards (although there will be forays into earlier periods in history when understandings of particular kinds of violence require it). I will also explore how violence in the modern world differs from the pre-modern world, and what is significant about those differences. That means understanding what violence is, and how its manifestations might vary from one region of the world to another. To understand those differences, past and present, I adopt the argument that violence is culturally relative so that in one part of the world an act can be considered an intolerable transgression by most members of that society, while in another part of the world and at the same time, that same act may be considered entirely legitimate. That is, violence is what a society acknowledges as violent; it is the difference between what is tolerated and what is not tolerated, between what is acceptable and not acceptable. The central question, as the historian Francisca Loetz has aptly put it, is not therefore, 'what is violence?', but 'What makes violence what it is in any given society?' That doesn't mean that violence is simply in the eye of the beholder, but it is an acknowledgement that it is best understood in particular, very specific cultural, social, economic, and political contexts.

## A question of definitions

No matter what specific act of violence one might be thinking about, it is almost certainly being carried out as these lines are being read. To understand violence—its meanings, its mechanisms, its functions, its uses—it is important to understand the world in which we live. Violence sheds light on the individual or groups who use it, but more broadly on the societies in which those individuals live, including the state and its institutions. Violence is, nevertheless, an ambiguous concept. Its definitional boundaries shift and change over time, depending on the cultural and political conventions of any given society. This is an important point. 'Violence' is often what a society perceives to be a violent act. Moreover, each sub-category of violence—rape, homicide, infanticide, massacre, genocide, and so on—has its own questions of definition and debates around what constitutes that particular kind of violence.

It is not unusual to find discussions on violence opening with the question, 'What actually *is* violence?' The answer is—it depends. That response might seem glib, so let me explain what I mean by looking at two definitions of violence, one quite narrow, the other broader in scope.

The first is by the Dutch criminologist Pieter Spierenburg, taking his cue from the anthropologist David Riches, who defined violence as 'an intentional encroachment upon the physical integrity of the body'. This idea of violence is limited to the physical infliction of harm on others and precludes things like the perpetration of psychological violence, or the psychological trauma experienced in the aftermath of violence.

A more comprehensive definition comes from the World Health Organization, which broadly defines violence as 'the intentional use of physical force or power, threatened or actual, against oneself, another person, or against a group or community, that either results in or has a high likelihood of resulting in injury, death, psychological harm, maldevelopment, or deprivation'. This definition considers violence to be more than just the physical transgression of the body; it is also about the harmful emotional and psychological after-effects that it produces.

In both definitions, the 'intentional' part is important; it precludes accidents (such as car accidents or accidental shootings), but includes most acts of violence encompassed by war, murder, rape, torture, corporal punishment, brawls, suicide, as well as state-sponsored violence. Neither of these definitions, however, includes the destruction of inanimate objects such as property or sites of cultural heritage that are often targeted during genocide, or indeed considers the untold harm done to animals and the environment by humans over the centuries.

Other scholars have been at pains to expand the definition of violence to include actions that were once never considered violent, but now are, including systems that maintain people in coercive, exploitative relationships, such as slavery and forced labour; human trafficking in people and body parts; the slow and utterly unspectacular grind of poverty that can lead to disease and premature death; and the overexploitation and degradation of the environment. Broader categories such as racism, incarceration (along with the physical and mental violence that can entail), death from preventable accidents or disease, abuse, and cruelty towards animals, the industrialized killing of animals for consumption, as well as bullying, humiliation, and verbal abuse (especially if it results in self-harm or suicide), are also now regarded as forms of violence by some scholars. These broader categories of violence question the notion of intent, that is, scholars who adopt a broad definition of violence often argue that it cannot be reduced to a corporal experience and that the outcomes produced by a violent action are often unintentional. A violent action is generally calculated, but its consequences are often unforeseen.

We can see just how difficult it can be to try and precisely define what is violence. Some of the broader categories of violence that have been mentioned will not be taken into consideration in this short introduction. As a result, I will have to bypass some of the leading thinkers on those forms of violence, such as the Norwegian sociologist Johann Galtung, who first formulated the idea of structural violence, the French sociologist Pierre Bourdieu, who developed the idea of symbolic violence, and the Slovenian philosopher Slavoj Žižek, who makes a distinction between what he calls 'subjective' (highly visible) and 'objective' (invisible) violence. All three question the notion of intent, arguing that violence cannot be reduced to a corporal experience and that the outcomes produced by a violent action are often unforeseen and unintentional.

For the purposes of this short introduction, I have adopted what some may deem a narrow definition of violence. I am going to limit my discussion to **acts born of a conscious desire to intentionally harm another person, group, or community, resulting in either physical injury or death**. I have, therefore, focused on the more visible, physical acts of violence—interpersonal, gendered, communal, religious, sexual, criminal, and political—at the expense of other forms of non-physical violence, which will only be touched on in the last chapter of the book.

## Approaches to violence

There are differences not only in defining violence but also in methodological approaches to studying it, depending on the discipline in question. Evolutionary psychologists, socio-biologists, anthropologists, archaeologists and bioarchaeologists, psychologists and psychiatrists, criminologists, as well as historians, sociologists, and political scientists have all put forward theories about violence ranging from its origins in early hominins and animals, to contemporary theories surrounding its causes, meanings, and aftermaths. Across many disciplines, the debates still revolve around the binary of whether humans are innately violent, that is, whether violence is part of our evolutionary and genetic make-up, or whether it is contingent upon cultural and historical context.

For evolutionary psychologists, violence is rooted in the deep prehistoric past; it is a biological mechanism that has evolved over centuries. Our aggressive impulses flowed from the need to acquire food, other scarce resources, and mates, and to avoid predators, thereby assuring the continued survival of the species. Evolutionary thinking on violence posits a number of biological drives (or motives) that explain violence because of genes or hormones. Aggression, for example, becomes a means to achieve a particular goal such as food, shelter, or sex. Genes don't make us violent; they simply contain the propensity for violence. Evolutionary theory, according to Azar Gat, cuts through the 'nature versus nurture' debate on violence by postulating that aggression is a tactical skill—both innate *and* learned. That is, the environment plays a significant role in mediating gene expression. It explains why, according to this theory, some societies are more violent than others, depending on the environment in which humans were raised. Some evolutionary theorists go so far as to argue that specific physical traits were developed and selected over time to ensure the survival of the species. Thus, for example, the fist and the face, according to one study, supposedly evolved to both inflict injury and to minimize injury from punches during fights between males.

Evolutionary psychology has been critiqued by the likes of biological psychologists Antonio Damasio and David J. Buller, who both point out that natural selection does not lead to homogeneous psychological traits. Buller argues that the human brain would have undergone significant change over the past 100,000 years, something that some evolutionary psychologists don't accept. However, the debates around biology or culture as prime drivers of violence appear increasingly redundant as scientists accept the role of culture, and historians increasingly accept the role biology can play in shaping human behaviour in the past.

The other means by which scholars have attempted to draw links between the present and our earliest ancestors is to compare them with what are termed 'pure' hunter-gatherer societies from the recent past, such as Aboriginal Australia or the Amazon. Among these people, it is argued, there are very high rates of homicide, much higher (statistically speaking) than that of industrialized societies. Some anthropologists extrapolate from the study of these groups to suggest that 'pure' hunter-gatherers must be like hunter-gatherers in prehistory, and that homicide rates among them must also have been as high.

Using data about present-day hunter-gatherers to make inferences about our prehistoric past is, for some, a questionable approach, but these studies feed into the ongoing debate in anthropological circles between those who argue that early humans were very violent, and that pre-agricultural societies were always at war, and those who contest such blanket characterizations and argue that there was little violence among early hunter-gatherers. The first view was common among anthropologists and archaeologists until the 1996 publication by Lawrence Keeley, *War Before Civilization*, a seminal work which sparked a wave of new research and a debate that continues to this day. Keeley made a convincing case for the existence of conflict and inter-group warfare in prehistory, debunking so-called anthropological 'myths' about peaceful hunter-gatherers, by examining the archaeological evidence in a different way.

Other anthropologists, such as Douglas Fry and Brian Ferguson, have questioned Keeley's assumptions and argue that hunter-gatherers were more inclined to avoid interpersonal as well as inter- and intra-group violence and that, overall, they lived peaceful lives. According to these scholars, violence and 'warfare'—defined broadly as socially organized, collective, deadly aggression between two or more groups—only came after humans developed sedentary lives with the invention of agriculture some 12,000 years ago. The crux of this debate is around definitions of warfare, and the question of 'culture', which, put simply, means that you had to have something to fight about (or for), and not just scarce resources. In this view, warfare is an invention of complex, stratified societies. There is now a growing consensus that intergroup violence (warfare) existed in nearly all prehistoric societies, but debates around its frequency, nature, role, and significance continue to take place.

Then there is the archaeological record. There are two kinds of objects that archaeologists and bioarchaeologists examine when determining whether violence has occurred in the deep past: rock art that depicts inter-group violence; and skeletal evidence that points to violent trauma (head injuries, bone fractures), or a weapon lodged in or found close enough to human bone to lead to the conclusion that it was the cause of death. It is, however, notoriously difficult to interpret rock art, and just as difficult to determine whether physical damage on a skeleton was caused by fighting, an accident, or some ritual that has been lost in time. Although several 'massacre sites' have been found in parts of Europe and Africa for the Mesolithic and Neolithic periods (interestingly, nothing yet has been found for these periods in South-East or East Asia), there are no cave paintings of group conflict or skeletal remains of traumatic violence from the Palaeolithic (representing most of human existence).

The current debates regarding hunter-gatherers mirror in some respects the old debates around the works of Thomas Hobbes (1588–1679) and Jean-Jacques Rousseau (1712–78). Hobbes believed that all interpersonal relations were violent, and that violence was a natural and inevitable part of social life. Rousseau believed that 'natural man' was in essence peaceful and was corrupted by civilization. Neither of these positions is tenable; humans are not one or the other. Humans are capable of violent outbursts and brutal behaviour, but we are also capable of cooperation and collaboration. Indeed, society can only exist when the vast majority of interpersonal relations are free of violence.

Sociologists often look to history to help explain violent human behaviour. The three most influential theorists on violence do this—Max Weber (1864–1920), Norbert Elias (1897–1990), and Michel Foucault (1926–84). I will come back to them intermittently in the following pages but note that these theorists of violence, upon whom scholars rely heavily in formulating their own interpretations, are western European. They have been so central to understanding violence in the modern world that it has resulted in a very western-centric approach. It is time to rethink our understanding of violence in the non-western world, but, given the limited space, not here. The most I can do is to try and incorporate scholarship, when and where possible, from other eras and cultures.

Weber, Elias, and Foucault each had very different approaches to understanding violence, even if they all understood and linked violence to the history of punishment and the state. Weber believed that politics was about power, and that power was ultimately grounded in coercive violence. The state was a coercive institution that had managed to gain what he called a 'monopoly of violence' over the centuries. Elias argued that over the course of time, and in parallel with the development of more complex judicial systems and policing, elite notions of masculine behaviour evolved into a general disdain of interpersonal violence as no longer compatible with 'civilized' behaviour. It was only by 'internalizing' instincts, and in particular aggression, that civilization could follow. Elias thus linked the rise of the state to the development of self-control—the mastery of impulsivity. Foucault argued that pre-modern states used the body as a stage on which to perform violence, such as spectacular public executions, to overcome any resistance to their centralizing impulses, and to reinforce the state's legitimacy. Punishments had to be spectacular spectacles because there was no other way of enforcing the law. That violence, according to Foucault, eventually gave way to another kind of disciplinary power—prisons, barracks, schools, and factories.

Violence in the western tradition is thus posed as a problem that can be solved by applying rational thought. This kind of thinking can be found in the likes of Elias, or more recently in the work of Harvard psychologist Steven Pinker, who argue that violence is the exact opposite of civilization or of rationality. For historians and some historical sociologists, by contrast, violence is almost never senseless, and it is almost never irrational; it always has a purpose and a function even if it is not immediately obvious to the outside observer. That doesn't mean to say that violence cannot be irrational but that all acts of violence, even the seemingly irrational such as road-rage, the lone gunmen with mental health issues, or football hooligans, can be explained.

For many sociologists and criminologists, violence is about power—power to inflict injury, power to impose one's will on and to dominate another, and the power to resist (violence can be deployed by the powerless against the powerful). For historians, the distinction between 'legitimate' and 'illegitimate' forms of violence can be so blurred as to become meaningless. This was the case, for example, when Brownshirts carried out what was referred to as the 'people's justice' by publicly humiliating and shaming Jews, or women who had slept with Jews, on the streets in 1930s Germany. There were Nazis in government who did not necessarily approve of the Brownshirts' behaviour, but it was tolerated since it was the kind of exclusionary violence that contributed towards the creation of a racial state. Another example was the American soldiers at Abu Ghraib who abused and tortured with the knowledge and approval of their political and military superiors. Some of the techniques they practised dated back to the Cold War. It would be difficult to call these examples of violence 'legitimate' in any normative sense.

In both examples, individuals may 'know' they are committing an act of violence but think that it is perfectly acceptable, that the circumstances require it even. The distinction between 'legitimate' and 'illegitimate' then says a good deal more about the nature of the law or state power than it does about the nature of violence, since it often neglects the obvious question—who decides what is legitimate and what is illegitimate? The problem is complicated even further when the notion of 'legitimate' is broadened to embrace violence as a useful instrument to achieve 'just ends'—by overthrowing a tyrannical polity, ousting a colonial oppressor, or dismantling exploitative structures and institutions. In those instances, violence can arguably become a moral imperative and in the process become redemptive.

Two very different approaches to historicizing violence appeared during the 1970s and 1980s. The first approach emerged out of cultural history, exemplified by people like Natalie Zemon-Davis, who in 1973 published a ground-breaking study on 'the rites of violence' in 16th-century France. Davis was able to throw light on behaviours that historians until then had dismissed as seemingly irrational acts of barbarism or savagery by interpreting them in terms of their social-symbolic significance. She created a paradigm for a great deal of the cultural analysis of violence that was to follow. The other approach emerged out of the social history of crime, with people like James Sharpe, one of if not the first person to use the term 'history of violence' in the English language. Sharpe, along with several other English historians of the 1980s, focused on the criminal courts in the early modern period, attempting to trace statistically the decline of violence by looking at homicide rates. This trend is best exemplified by the work of the Cambridge criminologist Manuel Eisner.

These two approaches—one centred on understanding the meanings of violence and the symbolism attached to it, the other based on quantitative methodology—have continued to the present day. There is admittedly not always a clear-cut distinction between the cultural and the criminological—they sometimes overlap—but they broadly represent the two dominant methodological currents in the history of violence, creating two very different trajectories with two very different objectives. Scholars who are preoccupied with rates of different kinds of violence—homicide, in particular, but also deaths in war, as well as rape figures, domestic abuse figures, and so on—tend to argue for an overall decline in violence.

However, measuring some of these kinds of violence, as we shall see, can be problematic. There are not only issues of definition (what constitutes homicide or rape can vary enormously from one historical period and from one legal jurisdiction to another), but the trustworthiness of some of the data is debatable, while the statistics are always open to interpretation. Important as it is to get a sense of patterns, trends, and variations across time and place, most forms of intimate violence are hidden from view and remain grossly under-reported to the authorities. Moreover, quantifying violence does not necessarily give an accurate portrayal of overall levels of violence in a society at any given time. On the other hand, scholars who are preoccupied with cultural interpretations of violence look to understand its meanings and forms. It often becomes a tool of communication and representation, whether considered legitimate or not, and it is often tied to notions of masculinity.

Most of what I look at in the following pages places specific forms of violence within a larger cultural context. The context is not a causal explanation for violence, but it helps us to understand the conditions in which it is perpetrated or practised. The underlying assumption is that to understand violence, one must analyse the ideas, values, and cultural practices embedded in the act. So, when reading about violence in this book, don't think of it as a single act or event, but as the outcome of a process that is always dependent on the personal, social, cultural, religious, and political context in which it takes place.

## How violent was the past?

There is a common (mis)perception that people in the ancient, medieval, and early modern worlds were brutal and violent, that they were desensitized to death, quick to anger, and all too ready to resort to violence to resolve disputes. The further one goes back in time, the more violent it was supposed to have been.

This is the kind of thinking one can find in recent works by political scientists John Mueller, Azar Gat, and Joshua Goldstein, and the evolutionary psychologist Steven Pinker. They all postulate the decline in violence over the centuries by pointing to a diminution in conventional warfare and deaths in war, especially in the 20th century, and to the decline in homicide rates in Western European countries from peaks in the 13th century to the relatively low rates today. They tend to use homicide rates in western Europe, where record keeping was more or less accurate, and deaths in warfare, to draw conclusions about overall levels of violence in any given society.

This is a view that is contested, so I'll come back to it later, but it is worth pointing out that almost none of the authors who hypothesize a decline in violence—with the exception of Pieter Spierenburg, at the crossroads of history, criminology, and sociology—are historians. The disparity in understandings usually centres on historical interpretations of the past and the use of statistics to demonstrate the extent of the violence. Pinker and Eisner, for example, use statistics to posit a view of the pre-modern world as brutal and bloody, a world that was transformed from the mid-17th century onwards into one in which interpersonal violence became increasingly unacceptable, and state displays of violence, such as public executions, were no longer considered to serve an educative purpose so that they eventually disappeared. A process of 'civilization', in part brought about by the Enlightenment, is meant to have transformed the ways in which people thought about and reacted to violence. It is no coincidence that this happened in the 18th century, at the same time as the concept of 'natural rights' and ideas about human rights and human dignity were beginning to emerge.

Those who contest the decline thesis argue that the past is often made out to be more violent than it was, especially in popular culture. The decline thesis only really works if world history is divided into two phases: before the Enlightenment, the world was superstitious, cruel, and violent; after the Enlightenment the world was rational and more peaceful. No one contests the idea that the pre-modern world was violent. Medieval law recommended public executions, burning, branding, blinding, drowning, and castration for felonies. The use of judicial torture and spectacular uses of public execution were common in Europe from the 15th to the 18th century. As a matter of historical fact, however, scholars cannot say with any certitude that people in the pre-modern world were 'more violent' or 'less violent' than we are today. The medieval historian, Warren Brown, for example, has concluded that 'thirteenth-century England as a whole was not significantly more violent than the US or EU around the turn of the twenty-first century'.

That precept—that people in previous centuries were no more violent than we are today—guides our thinking about violence and the past. Take prehistory as an example. There is limited material evidence in the archaeological record for physical violence in the deep past, but it does exist. There are a couple of notable sites pre-dating the Agricultural Revolution, which in the Middle East occurred some 12,000 years ago. A site in present-day Croatia known as Sandalja II that dates from 27,000 years ago contains the remains of 29 people with their skulls smashed. At Jebel Sahaba, now in northern Sudan, a cemetery that dates from around 13,000 years ago consists of 61 individuals, some of whom had been killed by arrows. The archaeological evidence for violence is much more widespread after the Agricultural Revolution. Some of the largest sites found come from Central Europe, such as Asparn-Schletz in Austria, where the remains of over 200 individuals have been found; most of the skulls had lethal fractures.

Scholars conclude from this and similar archaeological evidence from prehistory that our own species (*Homo sapiens sapiens*) fought and killed each other during the Upper Palaeolithic

(50,000–10,000 years ago), that violence occurred between groups (inter-group violence), and that violence occurred between individuals within groups (intra-group violence). Warfare and violence came to humans quite early on, before agricultural settlements and before cities existed; people killed and massacred, even if the reasons they did so cannot be known with any certitude. It is, however, impossible to draw any overarching conclusions from the existing archaeological record about the extent of violence in the deep past. A recent study on prehistoric Japan, for example, concluded that violence, including warfare, was *not* common.

There is a recognition that violence was an integral part of social life in previous centuries, depending on the epoch being discussed, but there is reason to believe that life was not as violent as has been made out in the media and in film. Forms of violence, as well as rates of violence, varied enormously over time and from one region of the world to another. But as we shall see, all past societies were differently violent. That is, violence was used differently in different situations, according to what was considered acceptable and what was not. The question then is not 'how violent was such and such a period', but rather, 'how was such and such a period violent?'

# Chapter 2
# Intimate and gendered violence

The family is probably one of the most violent social institutions in the world and has been throughout history. In many societies in the past, if a wife disobeyed or displeased her husband, he had the right to discipline her. The same rule applied to parents disciplining their children. It was not until the 19th century that what is called intimate and gendered violence began to be questioned, and that legislation to protect women and children began to be introduced, requiring the intervention of the law. Most forms of intimate and gendered violence are carried out by men against women and children (or men in same sex relationships) and can include things like domestic violence, sexual assault, and child sexual abuse (both institutional and familial). This violence is still accepted and is indeed endemic in many parts of the world today—in Africa, Latin America, the Middle East, and parts of Asia—and is intimately tied to male attitudes. The exception to this rule is infanticide, where women are predominantly the perpetrators, although sometimes with the complicity of their male partners. Women can be perpetrators in other kinds of intimate violence—they can abuse their partners and their children, for example—but they are statistically always in the minority.

## Domestic violence

In most cultures throughout history, if a wife disobeyed her husband, it was thought right and proper that she should be 'corrected'. There is enough research to suggest that this kind of violence was such an integral part of marriage in pre-modern Europe that there is little trace of domestic abuse in the archives. It often only comes to our attention in court records when disciplining resulted in permanent injury, miscarriage, or death. In Europe in the ancient and medieval worlds, male heads of households were entitled, indeed expected, to employ physical force to keep discipline among those under their control. The problem in the past was not the act of assault itself, but how to distinguish between 'acceptable' levels of violence and excessive force.

It was only in the 19th century that wife-beating, along with other forms of physical violence like street fighting, came to be viewed as unacceptable, and as a predominantly working-class behaviour that had to be stamped out. In one data set on Victorian England compiled by historian Shani D'Cruze, more than one-third of those prosecuted for wife-beating were categorized as skilled workmen, around half as unskilled workers, and the rest as lower-middle-class. It was, however, still acceptable to 'chastise' children. When men nonetheless used excessive violence—defined as such if death or serious injury occurred—it could damage their social status.

Of course, then and now, statistics on intimate interpersonal violence like domestic abuse and sexual assault are extraordinarily difficult to collate since the violence is so under-reported and consequently largely hidden. Women do not want to prosecute their husbands for a whole array of reasons, consistent with women's reluctance to report sexual assault, including the way they are treated by the police and the judicial system, the low rates of conviction, and fear of further violence.

Domestic abuse rates vary enormously across the world. In Australia, which is on the lower end of the scale, in the early 21st century, one woman is killed on average every nine days, and one man every 29 days (the vast majority because of male-on-male violence). In 2016–17, 17 people were hospitalized every day because of an assault by a partner or another family member. Very similar rates of domestic violence exist for other affluent countries and much higher rates for other parts of the world. In economically developing nations, one in three married women is battered during her lifetime by her husband. Partner-perpetrated violence—which can be anything from beatings, enforced confinement, intimidation, economic and verbal abuse—is highest in the South-East Asian region at around 38 per cent, followed by the eastern Mediterranean (37 per cent), Africa (36 per cent), the Americas (30 per cent), Europe (25 per cent), western Pacific (24 per cent), and high-income countries (23 per cent), which comprise Australia, New Zealand, the United States, Canada, members of the European Union, Israel, South Korea, and Japan. In China today, where patriarchal values persist, and female submissiveness is still expected, domestic violence is largely accepted; women do not report beatings to the police for fear of upsetting 'family harmony'. To do so might provoke the disdain of the larger community. Patriarchal attitudes that can endanger women cut across the religious divide. In Christian communities, scripture can be used to justify domestic violence. The situation is similar in Muslim communities where the Qur'ān is sometimes used to justify oppressive practices towards women, a situation complicated by the intersection of religion (shari'a law) and the state in Muslim societies across Africa, Asia, and the Middle East. As sociologist Lisa Hajjar has noted, the most important issue for understanding domestic violence and impunity in Muslim societies is the relationship between religion and the state, a relationship that can vary widely across the Muslim world.

There are a number of socio-economic factors that have to be taken into account when explaining domestic violence. They include economic inequality; the predominance of patriarchal values or other forms of social inequality; social acceptance of violence in resolving domestic disputes; and the inability of women to leave violent family settings. All those things are preconditions for domestic violence, but it can only occur often if there is a degree of legal or social impunity involved in the act itself. When the perpetrator is not, for whatever reason, actively pursued and prosecuted by the law, it is often because male violence in a family setting is tolerated. This suggests a reluctance in many societies to recognize family violence *as violence*, or, to put it another way, family violence is considered legitimate.

There is also the act itself. Although it is difficult to make generalizations—circumstances will vary from one case to the next—the violence committed by the perpetrator is about demonstrating their power over the victim. The victim is being hurt, frightened, shamed, abused. The perpetrator is communicating to the victim, through an act that inflicts pain or control, that they 'own' and dominate them. Random violence can also create a psychological dependence on the part of the abused partner.

## Sexual violence

Sexual assault is a global problem of immense proportions. As with domestic violence, there are no firm statistics on the number of rapes, for example. We do not know how many people are victims nor how many people are perpetrators. We do know that sexual assault is grossly under-reported. Non-reporting is particularly high among minority women, the poor and disenfranchised, sex workers, and men. In Australia, around 85 per cent of sexual assault cases are not reported. There are lots of reasons for this, from fear of not being believed to the stigma attached to being raped, from fear of revenge from the perpetrator to the embarrassment and the additional trauma associated with the police investigation and court case. Fewer than 5 per cent of reported cases in the United Kingdom end with the rapist being convicted, a figure similar to the United States. In Australia, it's about 10 per cent. As well, historically, there were ways of avoiding prosecution for rape. In England in the first half of the 20th century, men might plead guilty to common assault charges to escape a charge of rape. As a result, far fewer rapes appear in the historical record. In most cases, men get away with rape. In some countries, such as India, sexual assaults are tolerated to a degree because they take place behind closed doors.

If there has been a shift in public understandings in some parts of the world around the acceptability of violence against women, that shift does not appear to be reflected in the statistics on sexual assault. Some of the figures are staggering. One study by the World Health Organization (data exists for 80 countries) concluded that 35 per cent of women worldwide have experienced either physical or sexual violence in their lifetimes. That figure can vary between 23 per cent in high-income countries to almost 38 per cent in the South-East Asia region. In India, a woman is raped on average every 20 minutes. In South Africa, where the magnitude of rape and gang rape has been called an 'unacknowledged civil war', it's every 36 seconds.

There are indications, however, that while some forms of violence like homicide have remained steady in many countries over the past 200 years, indecent assaults on women have increased, and dramatically so. In England, according to historian Clive Emsley, they rose from almost 3,000 reported assaults in 1940–4, to over 11,000 in 1965–9. Similarly, in the United States, there has been an increased rate of reporting from 21,000 in 1964 to well over 100,000 in 1992 (numbers steadily declined after 1992, rising again to over 130,000 in 2016–18). This may be the result of an increased awareness of assault as a societal problem, and an increased willingness among the police to take assault seriously, as well as broader definitions of sexual abuse and assault. It is nevertheless difficult to determine the extent to which reports have increased because of a rise in assaults or an increased preparedness on the part of victims (men and women) to report them; it's probably a bit of both. In affluent countries at least, the taboo around discussing violent sexual and predatory behaviour in public appears to be diminishing. Regardless of the increased awareness around issues of sexual violence and sexual harassment—the #MeToo movement has been a global phenomenon—myths and stereotypes around rape persist. Historian Joanna Bourke has highlighted three of those myths.

The first is the belief that 'women lie' about sexual assault. It's a myth that is deeply embedded in our society, particularly within police forces and criminal justice systems. One 2008 survey of 891 police officers in the south-eastern United States found that more than 50 per cent of officers believed that half of women who complained of rape were liars and 10 per cent believed that the majority of complainants were lying. A second myth is that a woman can only get pregnant if she is consenting. In other words, if a woman is raped and gets pregnant, it can't have been rape. This is an archaic view that still has proponents today. In a 2012 interview, United States Senator Todd Akin referred to some rapes as 'legitimate'. The third myth is the idea that the victim 'had it coming to her'. Rapists routinely state that their victims were seductive, perhaps by wearing revealing clothing, and therefore at fault. Both men and women believe this. In a recent poll in the United Kingdom, one-third of women stated that if a woman was being flirtatious, it was somehow her fault if she was raped. The reality is that men often force themselves onto women and later claim they were consenting. When someone says that an act is 'rape' or 'sexual abuse', a large degree of scepticism still prevails both in societies at large and in legal institutions; the onus is placed on the victim to prove that they have been assaulted.

This brings us to legal definitions of rape, which can vary enormously from one period to another, from one country to another, and even within countries when there are different legal jurisdictions. The meaning of rape will thus vary greatly across socio-cultural settings. It is also a contested category that can include male on male sexual violence, something I won't explore here, in part because it is so under-researched, but also because for most of history, rape was defined as forceful penile penetration of the vagina, in the absence of a woman's consent, by a man who was not the woman's lawful husband. That is, rape within marriage, child rape, or male rape was not recognized. Rape in marriage, for example, did not become a crime until late into the 20th century—marital rape was only recognized in Scotland in 1989 and in the rest of the United Kingdom in 1992—and is still not recognized as a crime in some 50 countries in the world today (including Bangladesh, China, India, Saudi Arabia, and Yemen), especially where dowries are involved, which implies the wife is bought and is therefore property. Despite the laws in many countries, between 10 per cent and 26 per cent of women experience rape in marriage, depending on the part of the world they live in.

Rape-in-marriage law reforms in the western world in the second half of the 20th century, brought about by women's shifting status in modern society, were not achieved without controversy. There was, and still is in some parts of the world, opposition to the idea that it should be a criminal offence for a husband to sexually assault his wife. At its core is the idea that the state should not intervene in the family home, and especially in the marital bedroom. This is ironic given that the same groups who opposed rape-in-marriage law reform—social and political conservatives, some religious groups, and even conservative women's groups—often opposed legalizing homosexuality.

As with domestic violence, rape thrives in situations of social and economic inequality. In her work on the history of the rapist, Joanna Bourke argues that rape is a form of social and political performance, that it is highly ritualized, and that sexual violence is deeply rooted in specific cultural, social, and political contexts.

## Child sexual abuse

Child sexual abuse is the involvement of a child in sexual activity, or the exploitation of a child through prostitution or pornography. As with other forms of intimate and gendered violence, knowledge about sexual violence against children in the past is limited by the state of the records, and the unwillingness of parents or people in authority to report or even believe children who talked about their experiences. As a result, sexual assault against minors, much like rape, is grossly under-reported. Violence against children, whatever the nature of that violence, rarely results in an arrest or conviction. Despite articles in the press in recent years around institutional abuse in the western world, and despite a good deal of work done on the subject since the 1980s, there has been almost no historical research on child sexual abuse in many regions of the world.

By the 1980s, child sexual abuse was widely recognized in most western nations as a serious social problem. It was in part the result of media attention around various forms of abuse, including child pornography, paedophile rings, and sex-murders. There was also an increasing awareness of the rates of intra-familial sexual assault. During the 1980s, reports of all forms of child sexual abuse in the United States swelled, in part due to widening definitions. In the United States, 22 per cent of Americans had allegedly been victims of child sexual assault, while in Britain it was claimed that one in 10 children had been sexually assaulted. This led to an increase in policing, social work, and institutional resources for children, families, and caseworkers. South Africa has one of the worst records. The Tears Foundation and the Medical Research Council have stated that 50 per cent of South Africa's children will be abused before the age of 18.

Sexual activity with 'a minor' is *by definition* 'violent'. There are two interrelated problems that complicate the question of child sexual abuse—the age of consent, and the legal definition of a 'minor', that is, a person who has not reached a designated stage of maturity. Such variations are linked to ideas about the onset of puberty; different expectations of childhood; shifting views about the innocence or culpability of infants and youth; and the strength of feminist and other activist movements. Historically, the age of consent has varied enormously from one part of the world to the next, and indeed still does. In England and Wales, for instance, the age of consent was raised from 12 to 13 years of age in 1875, then, scarcely 10 years later, to 16 years. There was no corresponding 'age of consent' for boys, although it now varies in many countries from between 16 and 18 years of age. In the United States, by the end of the 19th century, the difference between the age in which a girl's 'yes' was deemed legally to be meaningful could be as young as 10 in Mississippi and Alabama and as high as 18 in Kansas and Wyoming. In many parts of the world today, marriage overrides the age of consent and renders sex between a husband and a child legal, regardless of the age of the child.

Even in countries where a minimum age of marriage has been fixed at 18, legal loopholes can be found. According to the international not-for-profit *Girls Not Brides: The Global Partnership to End Child Marriage*, in Morocco, judges approve 90 per cent of the requests they receive to let minors marry. Likewise, in Tanzania, a girl can be married at 15 with the consent of her parents. Almost one in 10 children in some countries in East Asia are married by the age of 15. In Bangladesh, over a quarter of girls are married before the age of 15. In Laos, for instance, 37 per cent of children are married before they turn 18, while in the Solomon Islands the figure is 28 per cent. The rate is even higher in some parts of Africa: in rural areas of northern Nigeria, it is estimated that 90 per cent of girls are married before they are 12 years old. As a result, there are at least 700 million child brides in the world who have been married before the age of 15.

Broadly speaking, scholars make a distinction between three different kinds of child sexual abuse: abuse committed by a stranger; abuse committed by people in authority known to the family carried out within institutions whose moral responsibility is to protect children; and abuse committed within the family—intra-familial sexual assault, commonly referred to as incest. There have been an increasing number of studies into the sexual abuse of children within institutions, including schools, orphanages, and religious bodies. This kind of violence was relatively common for much of the modern era, as government inquiries held in Canada (1996), Ireland (2000), the United States (2011), and Australia (2017) have demonstrated. In the case of the family, there have been significant complications with uncovering, policing, and prosecuting familial sexual violence. A great deal of secrecy surrounds violence within the family, both historically and into the present. Family sexual violence continues to remain largely hidden. As for institutional violence, organizations like the Catholic Church failed to support victims over long periods of time, while systematically protecting alleged perpetrators, including moving them to different parishes.

Sex trafficking, sex tourism, and child pornography are also widespread across the globe. UNICEF has estimated that over 1 million children are trafficked annually to the west from countries in South and South-East Asia, South and Central America, and eastern Europe, generally to work in the sex industry. (Other more conservative reports put the figure at around 600,000–800,000 children trafficked each year across international borders.) It is estimated that around 2 million children work in the sex trade in Asia alone.

The internet has become a site of child sexual exploitation in ways that never existed before the 21st century. Online trading and sharing of images and videos of children being sexually abused and tortured has increased dramatically over the last 20 years. Indeed, the problem has skyrocketed since 2014 when it was thought the number of images reached the million mark. As of 2018, tech companies identified over 45 million images and videos of children being sexually abused on the internet, some as young as 3 or 4 years of age, some even younger. Does that mean there are more paedophiles in the world, or simply that those inclined can get access to pornographic material more easily? Does that mean more children are being abused and assaulted than ever before? There is evidence of growing rings of child prostitution around the world, particularly in conflict zones such as Sierra Leone, where it is estimated that some 37 per cent of sex workers are aged under 15 years. Some regions have legislated to specifically combat sex tourism, but local enforcement agencies are often ineffectual.

## Infanticide

Infanticide is the killing of a baby at or shortly after birth by the mother (or at least generally with her knowledge). This too is a practice that has always existed but, as with other forms of intimate and gendered violence, it is impossible to give any accurate figures. Given the state of past medical knowledge, it was often impossible to determine for certain whether a newborn child had been born alive or dead. In recognition of the difficulties involved in determining the cause of death, authorities increasingly criminalized the concealment of the pregnancy. This was in the belief that a woman who did not publicly acknowledge her pregnancy and prepare for the child's care must have intended to kill the child. In the French city of Rennes, in 1721, after a fire had ravaged the town, 80 infant skeletons were found in the drains. The women who consigned their children's bodies to the drains of Rennes, and of other cities as well, were likely to have been servants or daughters living in households where they had been able to conceal their pregnancies but were unable to hide a newborn child. It is clear from testimonies given in court that neighbours, midwives, or family members did on occasion help single mothers conceal births and ensure that the newborn did not survive. This means that the convictions for infanticide or concealment of birth recorded by courts cannot be considered at all an accurate measure of the extent of the phenomenon. In other words, infanticide before the modern era went largely undetected.

It appears the sex of the baby was never a consideration, at least in Europe, and that it was generally about disposing of unwanted or illegitimate births, or a means of controlling family size. In Victorian London, hundreds of small bodies were found every year, but there was neither the willingness nor the resources to pursue the crime. One estimate by historian George Behlmer put the number of infanticides in England and Wales in the thousands every year, a figure that was and is never considered when calculating homicide rates. While the harsh penalties against infanticide enacted during the 16th and 17th centuries continued into the modern era in many places, in others they were eased as courts became more willing to give women the benefit of the doubt. In England by the 18th century, temporary insanity was being increasingly accepted as a plea in infanticide cases. This could still lead to a conviction, but it also held out the possibility of a pardon.

There were 196 trials at the Old Bailey in London between 1690 and 1799 for infanticide; only 62 of these returned guilty verdicts. Wider attitudes towards women began to shift in the 18th century when courts were more prepared to consider the mental state of the women in question (and of murderers in general). As such, women who killed their children were often cast in the roles of victims or they were increasingly seen to be insane. By the mid-19th century, a woman who was tried for child-murder in England would escape execution and be convicted instead of a misdemeanour.

If the sex of the baby doesn't appear to have been a consideration in Europe, this was not the case in other parts of the world—such as China, India, Vietnam, Pakistan, and Azerbaijan—where the pressure to produce a male child meant and still means that many female children are killed or abandoned. Let's look at two examples, India and China.

It is often reported in the media that the most dangerous place in the world to be a girl is in India. Apart from the danger of rape, there are significant issues surrounding female infanticide and female foeticide (the selective abortion of girls in the womb). Although infanticide has been illegal since 1870, it continues because of extreme poverty, unwanted children conceived after rape, children with a disability, children born to impoverished families, unmarried mothers, and the dowry system. Although the state has taken steps to abolish the dowry system, the practice persists, and for poorer families in rural regions female infanticide and gender selective abortion are attributed to the fear of being unable to raise a suitable dowry and then being socially ostracized.

Similarly, female infanticide has existed in China for centuries. As in India, the main causes were a patriarchal society, a dowry system, and poverty. As a result, infanticide was widespread, despite both Buddhist and Confucian precepts against the practice. In 19th-century China, drowning was a common method used to kill female children, as were suffocation, starvation, and exposure to the elements, despite the fact that, as historian Michelle King has pointed out, male Chinese elites considered infanticide a 'vulgar custom'. In 1979, in a radical social experiment, the Chinese government introduced the One Child Policy with the intention of keeping the population within sustainable limits. It seems to have exacerbated this centuries-old tradition of a preference for sons. In a society that was already highly patriarchal, many parents believed that having a son was vital in providing for them in their old age. It is impossible to know how many girls may have been killed in this way—many villagers had girls but simply did not register them—but some estimates are in the millions.

## Sexual assault in times of war

Warfare, as Joanna Bourke reminds us, is more than just about 'engaging in mechanical slaughter'. Rape, sexual violence, sexual murder, and sexual torture in war have been committed throughout history but it is only in recent times that scholars (and the public) have begun to research and discuss these topics more openly. This was the result of a number of things: the revelations in the 1990s about mass rapes and 'rape camps' during the war in the former Yugoslavia, as well as the sexual violence during the genocide in Rwanda; the confessions about 'comfort women' in Asia during the Second World War; and the research that has come to light about Soviet mass rapes in Eastern and Central Europe during the same war. It is possible that more rapes occurred during the Second World War than during any other war. As there is much more research on rape perpetrated in wartime against women and girls than rape committed against men and boys, I'll limit the following remarks to heterosexual assaults.

Before the 1990s, rape in warfare was not all that much discussed, partly because the men and women who were victims didn't talk much about it. There are reasons for the silence. Victims can feel a sense of shame for what they have experienced, while remembering can be painful, especially when the account touches on deeply traumatic and personal events. The 16-year-old Gabriele Köpp, for example, was one of an estimated 2 million women raped by the Red Army as it made its way across eastern Europe near the end of the Second World War; half of them may have been gang raped. Köpp did not write of her harrowing experiences until the age of 80 and was only the second German woman to do so. It has been estimated that as a result of the rapes, 10,000 women in Berlin alone committed suicide. The Soviets continued to rape German women for years after the war to the point where it became a 'political' problem for the newly founded German Democratic Republic (Figure 1).

1. **Soviet soldiers harass a German woman in Leipzig, Germany, August 1945.**

Rape is carried out by individuals associated with invading armies, regardless of the side they are on, regardless of the war. German soldiers and Nazis perpetrated sexual torture and rape during the war, including against Jewish women in ghettos, in concentration camps, and in war zones. The Allies raped in France and the

Philippines, in Italy and Japan during the Second World War. According to historian Bob Lilly's estimate, between 14,000 and 17,000 women were raped by American military personnel in Europe between 1942 and 1945. Thousands of Japanese women were raped in the years after the war, some of them by Australian and New Zealand soldiers who made up the British Commonwealth Occupation Force in Japan.

During the war, the Japanese army sexually enslaved tens of thousands of women, who have since become known by the euphemism 'comfort women', a problematic term that some scholars understandably consider demeaning. From the late 1930s, rape and enforced prostitution were a feature of the Japanese invasion of East Asia, although there were antecedents in the Siberian Intervention (1918–22). Estimates of the number of women forcibly taken or tricked into sexual slavery range from between 50,000 and 200,000, mostly Korean, but also Chinese, Taiwanese, Filipino, and some Japanese women. The Japanese military, unable or unwilling to devise a less brutal system, reasoned that comfort stations would reduce rapes of local women. The Japanese army was by no means the only one guilty of forcing women into prostitution during the Second World War. So too did the German military, with estimates of up to 50,000 women and girls kept in brothels throughout the German-occupied territories. The Nazis also set up brothels inside concentration and forced labour camps whose 'customers' were camp prisoners, part of a perverted reward system for some of the prison population.

Since the end of the Second World War, the catalogue of sexual violence in armed conflicts is significant and troubling. In 1947, the partition of Punjab between India and Pakistan led to between 75,000 and 100,000 women being kidnapped and raped. Over nine months during the Indo-Pakistani War in 1971–2, between 200,000 and 400,000 Bengali women were raped, 80 per cent of whom were Muslim. In the 1990s, there was widespread rape as well as torture and killings in Bosnia-Herzegovina, Kosovo, East Timor, Sierra Leone, and Guatemala. During the 1991–9 conflict in the former Yugoslavia, mass rapes took place on all sides, but systematic and widespread violations were perpetrated by Serbian forces against Muslim, Catholic, and Croatian women. According to some estimates, approximately 20,000 women were raped. Women and girls were routinely violated in their homes, incarcerated in detention camps established explicitly for the purpose of rape, and forced into prostitution. During the Rwandan genocide of 1994, between half and 90 per cent of surviving Tutsi girls and women were sexually assaulted, that is, anywhere between 250,000 and 500,000 women and children were raped. In the 21st century, mass rape in Darfur was an attempt to drive populations out of valuable land and into the desert. In 2011, one report estimated that in the Democratic Republic of the Congo, 1,000 girls and women were raped every day. One-third of victims were children under the age of 18 years.

Why rape occurs in warfare, and sometimes on a large scale, can vary from one theatre to another. In some theatres since 1945, rape appears to have become a deliberate tactic of war. We have seen this in the Congo and the former Yugoslavia where sexual violence became a 'weapon of war' that communicated a powerful message as an insult to the dignity of the enemy, and an act intended to humiliate the group. These examples are nevertheless rare. While men committing rape might not be driven by a desire to harm the community, they might be aware of the broader consequences of their actions. In these cases, to paraphrase Joanna Bourke, the penis is a weapon, it is a tool of violence and domination. In these instances, rape becomes a 'ritual' in which men bond through extreme violence (as with other atrocities). As has been pointed out by any number of scholars, the most important thing for men in warfare is the unit. It is these units or groups, central to life and survival in war zones, that often commit acts of extreme violence such as rape, rape-murder, torture, and massacre, regardless of orders they might have been given.

Where does all that leave us in terms of levels of gendered violence around the world? Gender violence appears to be on the rise in many parts of the world. There is no one cause behind this gender violence although outdated patriarchal and misogynistic attitudes can help in part to explain its prevalence. Violence against women and children, both in the family and outside it, persists to the present day and is an enormous global problem. In many communities around the world women and children are raped, trafficked, and exploited for their labour and as sex workers. The state oversees violence against women in conflict zones and sometimes systemically uses rape as a weapon of war both in communities and in refugee camps. Approximately one-third of all women around the world have at some stage in their lives been beaten and/or coerced into sexual relations. One-quarter of all pregnant women have experienced a form of domestic violence. According to a United Nations report, at least 200 million women and girls aged between 15 and 49 have experienced genital mutilation, sometimes referred to as clitoridectomy. There are still countries, such as Tanzania, Togo, Iraq, Kenya, and Ghana, where female genital mutilation is almost universal. It is thought that around 5,000 women are killed around the world each year in so-called 'honour killings'. All these measures are put in place to control female sexuality and female reproduction. Women are harassed and assaulted in the workplace at levels that are generally hidden from view and therefore carried out with impunity. I have only just touched the surface of the abuse women have to endure. Attitudes have shifted in some parts of the world but have gone nowhere near as far as they should, while they have barely shifted in many other parts of the globe. For the present, women are disproportionately the victims of sexual and domestic abuse in most societies around the world. The widespread evidence of sexual abuse, both in peace and in wartime, points to a disconcerting, widespread acceptance of rape that appears to be a factor in the very low rates of prosecution and conviction around the world.

# Chapter 3
# Interpersonal violence

For much of history, an act of male-on-male violence was as much about proving oneself in front of one's peers and belonging to a group as it was about the victim. This chapter will look at some of the reasons why men fight and kill, the kinds of violence used (feuding, the vendetta, knife fighting, duelling), how that violence is often bound up with what are called 'honour societies', and how over the centuries there has purportedly been a steady decline and transformation of interpersonal violence, especially in the western world.

I will outline some of the arguments used to explain the decline of murder in Europe and the United States. I am focusing on these two parts of the world for the simple reason that they are the two regions where scholars have a reasonably accurate, long-term picture of homicide. We are relatively ignorant about the prevalence of lethal interpersonal violence in the non-western world, largely because of a lack of research (although in some places, such as China, where record keeping goes back centuries, some pioneering work is being carried out). It will nevertheless be worth pointing to disparities in levels of male violence and the reasons they may be higher than in the western world. One of the questions I want to examine revolves around the apparent decline in the homicide rates in Europe over time, but not in the United

States. The two cases are somewhat different, and the arguments used to explain patterns in these countries are also different, but it goes to the question of why homicide rates can vary so dramatically from one country to another over time. If human capacity for violence is potentially the same, then why is it that some societies are more violent than others? What circumstances can lead to an increase in homicidal violence? Before I enter those debates, let's look at what are called honour societies.

## Changing notions of honour and the decline in violence

In many societies, both in the past and around the world today, a man's honour depends on his readiness to fight. Honour involves the esteem in which peers, or a society, hold an individual; it's often linked to physical strength and sexual prowess. Think of honour as an asset, in much the same way that property is, a value that men in particular set great store by. If one's honour is impugned, there is only one way of redeeming it, through retributive violence. External manifestations of one's masculinity—such as carrying a sword or a knife—were necessary in some cultures as a sign that one was prepared to defend one's honour. One could impugn a man's masculinity in any number of ways—a gesture, a look, an insult, an accusation of cuckoldry. That required the man to redeem his honour by proving his masculinity through an act of violence (with fist, staff, knife, or sword), which led to formal rituals of duelling in Italy, Spain, France, and England in the 16th century, as well as in Japan and India. Violence, form, and function, as historian Gerd Schwerhoff has argued, were thus intertwined in highly ritualized dramas that followed a clearly defined sequence of events—from teasing and insults to threatening gestures—that could end in serious injury and death. These dramas were usually played out in public; to leave a slight unanswered could lead to a loss of social standing not only for the individual but for the family.

Over time, the idea of honour was disassociated from the physical manifestations of bravery or masculinity, what Pieter Spierenburg dubbed the 'spiritualization of honour'. Honour increasingly became a personal, even a private affair, in which insults no longer automatically led to physical violence. This has to be seen alongside other developments in Europe from the end of the 17th century onwards: an increased emphasis on 'civility' and 'politeness' as alternatives to traditional concepts of male honour; the state legislating against fighting and duelling, along with the increasing opposition to duelling among elites as it became incompatible with 'civility'; and the development of judicial systems, an alternative to resolving disputes by force that could be accessed by a large number of people. In other words, declines in violence are also linked to changes in the way people interacted with and behaved towards one another.

These arguments are persuasive, but questions nonetheless remain. First, men who are obsessed with honour do not always express themselves through violence. Randolph Roth, for example, argues that honour does not explain why some societies are equally or consistently violent and believes honour to be 'a proximate cause of violence rather than the ultimate cause, a cultural vehicle for expressing deeper conflicts', such as economic interests, racial conflict, and social standing. Second, there may be no causal relation between civility and levels of violence. Although it is probably safe to say that there was an increasing intolerance towards some forms of physical violence, at least in Europe, since the early modern period, this does not mean that levels of violence decreased as a result of changing modes of social interaction. There was, after all, a revival in duelling in the 19th century in countries like Italy, Germany, and France. They were mostly middle-class men in the military who imitated the nobility in the hope of enhancing their social standing, but it appears the 'spiritualization of honour' had not completely taken hold in all classes of society.

Nevertheless, because of changing attitudes, some forms of violence appear to have diminished while others, such as domestic violence, simply became less public. At the same time, changing notions of masculinity and honour seem to have had an impact on attitudes towards violence, so that certain forms of punishment designed to publicly humiliate and demean the offender—such as the stocks, the pillory, and public floggings—declined during the 18th and into the 19th centuries. As historian Robert Shoemaker has pointed out, pillorying in England was abolished in 1837 because it came to be seen not to serve law and order, but to undermine it. In cases where the offender was deemed to have suffered an injustice—such as writers and printers for publishing illegal tracts—the crowds were very supportive. In those instances, the intention of the courts was undermined by sympathetic crowds. On the contrary, if the offender was convicted of an offence considered a transgression—fraud, blasphemy, and sexual offences like rape or bestiality—the crowd could turn violent, and in some instances assault and kill the offender.

## Homicide

Outside of warfare, homicide is one of the largest contributors towards violent deaths globally. Roughly 560,000 people died violent deaths in 2016 (excluding suicides). Fewer than 20 per cent of those individuals died in armed conflict, while around 68 per cent were the victims of intentional homicides. The number of homicides globally has been on the rise for the past three decades, from 362,000 deaths in 1990 to 464,000 deaths in 2017, but these are no more than rough estimates. Many states still do not produce data on violent deaths.

The basic result of the systematic study of homicide rates in European history, most notably by Manuel Eisner, is a picture of massive decline, from the end of the Middle Ages to the 1950s and 1960s. These days, scholarly claims for the decline in homicide are much more circumspect than they used to be. James Sharpe, for example, concludes that the generally accepted levels of homicide probably averaged about 20 in 100,000 in rural England in the 13th century, which dropped to around 1 in 100,000 by 1800 (the homicide rate is measured by deaths in 100,000 of population). Randolph Roth argues that the actual homicide rate in England in the early 1600s was probably around 15 in 100,000. Some scholars go so far as to argue that between the 13th and the 17th centuries the figures do not point to a 'consistent pattern of decline'. It is not until the 18th century, again largely because of record keeping, that historians can begin to make accurate generalizations about homicide rates in western Europe. By that stage, the homicide rate was about the same as it is today.

What we can say with a degree of certainty is that the real decline occurred from the 17th to the 18th century in a core set of western European countries—England, the Netherlands, Germany, and possibly France. That said, homicide rates remained relatively high in some Mediterranean countries—Italy, Spain, Greece—until later in the 19th century. Athens, for example, was the murder capital of the world at the end of the 19th century, at a time when there was a migrant influx from the countryside. By 1920, however, it had fallen to one of the lowest levels in the world, and indeed remains one of the least violent cities to this day. In China in the 18th century, on the other hand, one can observe the reverse trend, where homicide rates increased, largely as a result of the loss of central control by the Qing state, millenarian rebellions, piracy, and banditry. That trend was reversed in the 20th century so that today countries like China, Japan, Korea, and Singapore have some of the lowest homicide rates in the world. It is possible that the economic growth countries like Japan, Korea, and Singapore have experienced, without accompanying concentrations of poverty, may have a role to play, as well as the strong social stigma attached to arrest for crime in those societies. In other words, national and regional variations must be taken into consideration in any assessment of homicide rates, but just as importantly those discrepancies have to be accounted for.

Authorities in Europe up until the 16th century tended to look upon homicides that resulted from issues of honour or indeed of passion with a great deal of leniency. Only extreme cases of premeditated murder resulted in the death penalty. That began to shift between the 16th and 17th centuries when the settlement of a homicide was definitively taken out of the hands of the families concerned and kept in the hands of judges and sovereigns. It was during this time that homicide began to be seen as a crime, and people who committed homicide began to be seen as criminals. This is what Spierenburg refers to as the 'marginalization of homicide', which goes hand in hand with increasing social control that redefined the relationship between the state and its citizens. That is, declining homicide rates often occurred at times when there was a shift towards a broader acceptance of the state, seen as operating on behalf of its citizens, and capable of delivering justice. The marginalization of murder also corresponds with the argument advanced by the sociologist, Donald Black, that crime is a form of aggressive conflict management largely confined to low-status people who find themselves outside the law. In fact, they often consider the law repressive and removed from their daily experiences. They are consequently more likely to use aggression, including killing, to resolve their conflicts.

In other words, the decline in homicide does not necessarily correlate with the rise of the state, but it appears to have more to do with the relationship between the state and its citizens. In northern Europe, for example, the state was generally considered to be a legitimate institution that was designed to protect its citizens. In southern Europe, quite the opposite was happening, for a deep distrust between the people and state institutions developed. The same phenomenon can be observed in the United States. Randolph Roth argues that there have been four correlates of low rates of homicide in North America and western Europe over the past 450 years: the belief that government is stable and that its legal and judicial institutions will redress wrongs and protect lives and property; a feeling of trust in government and the officials who run it; empathy and fellow feeling arising from racial, religious, or political solidarity; and the belief that the social hierarchy is legitimate, that one's position in society can command the respect of others without resorting to violence.

When all these factors are in place, homicide can drop to as little as 1 in 100,000 people. Unlike other forms of interpersonal violence, there is a reasonably close correlation between the statistics and the actual crime, at least for the modern era. The seriousness of the crime means that it is more likely to be recorded than not. Nevertheless, many of the figures before 1800 are patchy and unrepresentative of any serious estimates of national homicide figures. Reduced rates in homicide are often used to postulate an overall decline in levels of violence, but there is considerable debate over the value and accuracy of crime statistics. In some cases, the statistics do not point to a correlation between low homicide rates and low levels of interpersonal violence.

A number of elements must be taken into account when formulating homicide rates, such as differing definitions of homicide across time and space, the manner in which a homicide is 'counted' (indictments, convictions, and so on), the willingness or not of states to record statistics, or even the willingness of police forces around the world to pursue investigations. One study of prosecutions in England since the 1850s, for example, suggests that coroners' budgets may have had something to do with the numbers prosecuted for murder. It is one of the reasons why infanticides are so often apparently overlooked or not pursued.

A report by the United Nations Office on Drugs and Crime divides homicide into three groups: interpersonal, criminal, and socio-political. Interpersonal homicide characterizes most homicides in affluent countries. Victim and perpetrator know each other and are often related. The murder of strangers is rare these days. Homicides related to organized crime are more common in regions like the Americas (North, South, and Central), and usually involve disputes over territory and control. Socio-political homicide is a category that includes civil terrorism, genocide, and hate crimes, and is a means of pursuing a political agenda. In the second and third categories, violence is a means of sending a message to others. 'People are killed', in the words of the report, 'for what they represent.' In other words, the victim's personal identity or experience is not relevant. The same might be said for the murder of LGBTQI people; it is not so much about their personal identity or experience as what they represent.

That said, there appears to have been little change in the sex and age structure of the vast majority of murderers over the centuries. Most homicides are committed by men in their reproductive prime (from their late teens to around the age of 40), usually against other men of the same age. This is a general rule for all time periods and all cultures (although there are exceptions to the rule). Perpetrators and victims are often of similar social status, often single, and, for the last 200 years or so, often belong to lower socio-economic groups. The only change in the profile of victims over the last 200 years is an apparent increase in the number of women victims. In Japan, Hong Kong, and China, for example, which have very low homicide rates (between 0.3 and 0.4 in 100,000 in 2011–12), women make up slightly over 50 per cent of homicide victims. The largest number of murders of women takes place in South Asia—Pakistan and India in particular. In India, around 40 per cent of homicide victims are women, but the figure is also high in countries like Austria, Germany, Norway, and Switzerland, again countries with very low homicide rates but where, respectively, around 40, 47, 47, and 50 per cent of homicide victims are women. Women and girls are, however, at greatest risk in Africa. In South Africa, about 3,000 women were murdered in the course of 2018—one woman every three hours. That is about the same number of women killed for the whole of Europe, with a population 12 times that of South Africa, in the same period, and more than five times higher than the global average.

Women who kill have made up around 5 to 10 per cent of the number of convicted murderers, depending on the region of the world, since at least 1900. The only apparent exception to the rule was early 18th-century Stockholm, where women made up about 45 per cent of murder and manslaughter offenders. This is one of the highest female participation rates found anywhere in the world and appears to be an aberration related to devout but suicidal women wanting to avoid eternal damnation. Instead of killing themselves, women preferred to kill somebody else, usually their own children, knowing full well that they would suffer the death penalty. Suicide would lead to hell; homicide, they believed, would lead to purgatory, after which they would be able to enter heaven.

Women mostly kill within their own domestic circle, but they were far more likely to be hanged than men, generally because their crimes were considered a greater threat to the social order, although there is no qualitative difference between male and female homicide. In England, between 1351 and 1826, females committing homicide were tried for 'petty treason', which would nominally be punished by burning at the stake. Men and women, in other words, were treated very differently, with men more likely to get off murder than women, although this trend appears to have changed by the second half of the 19th century. By that stage, women who killed, especially when they killed their violent husbands, although not treated leniently, were less likely to hang as an ideology of 'female innocence and weakness' emerged that required men to treat women more 'chivalrously'.

Before 1800, depending on the region and the period under consideration, homicide was a frequent enough occurrence and often involved notions of masculine honour. After 1800, in the western world at least, homicide ceased to be common and accepted, and became a 'sensational' act, an exception to the rule. Homicide rates may provide an indication of the degree to which violence was (or was not) kept within certain limits in any given society at any given time, but they do not necessarily offer an indication of overall levels of violence in a given society. Think too of deaths during times of war, normally excluded from homicide rates, or indeed the levels of violence that existed in 20th-century totalitarian societies with relatively low rates of homicide, but high levels of torture and death through incarceration in concentration camps and gulags. Those deaths were never accounted for in national homicide statistics. Nevertheless, homicide (and indeed interpersonal violence) in contemporary western Europe remains at a marginal level when compared to much of the rest of the world.

## The American exception

The United States is the exception to the industrialized world; Americans are two and a half to eight times more homicidal than people in any other affluent democracy. Two-thirds of the world live in countries that are less homicidal than America. There have been any number of reasons put forward to explain American gun violence but before considering them let's have a look at a few figures. In the five years between the shooting at Sandy Hook Elementary School in Connecticut in December 2012, which took the lives of 26 people, including 20 children aged between 6 and 7, and the school shooting in Parkland, Florida, in February 2018, in which 17 people were killed, America experienced 99 mass shootings, at least 239 school shootings, and at least 188,000 gun-related deaths (of which 8,000 were children under the age of 16). Every day, 100 Americans are killed by shooting and hundreds more wounded in gun violence. Every year, more American school-age children die from guns than on-duty police officers or military fatalities.

Those figures have to be broken down to be properly understood. Two-thirds of gun-related deaths are a result of suicide, that is, just one-third are homicides. Just as people are up to eight times more likely to be murdered in America, so too are people up to 10 times more likely to commit suicide than in most other affluent countries. The inverse relationship between homicide and suicide is not universal, but it is clear in many modern societies, and may have something to do with the internalization of concepts of male honour. Suicides now far outnumber homicides in most western countries, and as a global total of deaths compared to homicide. About 1 million people around the world commit suicide every year. Male suicide, as with male homicide, is much higher than female suicide and homicide, although for different reasons. Women are often better connected socially and have better support networks than their male counterparts.

As for homicides, black Americans represent the majority of victims, disproportionately killed by other blacks. In fact, black Americans are 10 times more likely to die from homicide by gun than a white American. Some of those black killings, admittedly a small percentage, involve police shootings, brought into the public consciousness through the Black Lives Matter movement. Police kill more people in America than in any other western country. In 2018, a total of 992 people were shot by American law-enforcement agents. (Roughly a quarter were black, half were white, and the rest were made up of other ethnicities. Police shootings are not included in homicide rates by the FBI.) Compare that with England where the number of people shot by police over a 10-year period between 2006 and 2016 came to a (still tragic) total of 23. English police are not generally armed and call on specially armed units when needed, but even when the figure is adjusted for population size, the death rate for police shootings is 64 times higher in the United States than in Britain.

The picture is complicated enormously by advances in policing and the medical sciences. Take the United States as an example. When non-fatal injuries due to firearms are taken into account, then the overall picture changes dramatically. In 2013, there were 84,258 non-fatal injuries. That brings the shooting statistic up to over 26 per 100,000 American citizens. Responses to the treatment of gunshot victims is better than at any other time in history, but there is also a tolerance for violence in America that is not found in any other affluent country. According to Roth, for various reasons, around three-fifths of killers in the United States escape punishment.

Attempts to explain the marked difference in homicide rates between America and the rest of the affluent world range from the historian Richard Slotkin's attempt to map the American national character and what he has dubbed the 'myth of regeneration through violence', through to the role of slavery and violence in the south, to arguments around democracy, gender, masculinity, and honour. Some social scientists even argue that homicide and suicide rates are higher in states that vote for Republican candidates for president than in states that vote for a Democratic candidate. None of these arguments is particularly convincing.

It's difficult to talk about homicide rates in America without mentioning what some have dubbed its 'gun culture'. America has a far larger proportion of households that own a gun (nearly half of all households) than any other country in the world, with the possible exceptions of Israel and Switzerland. Of course, there are two different things going on here. In Israel and Switzerland, where conscription requires military personnel to have a gun, the state expects of its citizens certain duties and responsibilities. This is not the case in the United States where about 30 per cent of

Americans own a gun and where gun ownership is an individual choice, often construed as an act of self-protection *against* the state. Of the 30 per cent of gun owners, two-thirds own more than one gun. This is twice the rate of gun ownership in the next highest countries, France and Canada (neither exactly known for their elevated homicide rates). Not surprisingly, there appears to be a correlation between gun ownership and the propensity to use firearms, especially when it comes to domestic violence and suicide. As well, given the high proportion of Americans who own a gun, it is impossible to know whether the prevalence of gun ownership has a kind of heightening effect, undermining trust on any number of levels—citizens towards each other, law enforcement agents towards citizens, and vice versa. It is impossible to know the extent to which some gun homicides might occur because people assume the other person *might* have a gun.

The question is whether gun ownership offers a material or a cultural explanation for America's high homicide rate. A good deal has been written about the Second Amendment and the 'right of the people to keep and bear arms'. The prevalence of gun ownership does not always translate into a high homicide rate (as we can see with Israel and Switzerland). If you eliminate homicide by shooting in the United States, the murder rate will still be (slightly) higher than in any other western country. In other words, widespread gun ownership is not the only cause of America's high homicide rate, even if it amplifies it. The problem lies deeper than simple gun possession and is tied to both social and distinct cultural-ideological traits. Randolph Roth's argument about attitudes towards the state and the role of the individual in society, as well as the apparent emphasis on individual (masculine) honour, the tolerance for violence, and the notion of a culture of self-help may, in part at least, explain both higher homicide rates and higher levels of interpersonal violence in the United States than in the rest of the western world.

## And the rest of the world

The total number of homicides around the world is about 800,000 people per year. Murder rates may have declined in much of the industrialized world, but this is not the case for many other parts of the world, especially in Africa, Latin America, and even in some cities in the United States whose murder rates are as high as some particularly poor developing nations. Central America is another region undergoing a crisis that threatens, in some respects, the foundations of the state and democratic government. In Mexico, the so-called drug wars have resulted in death rates second to only one other country in the world, Syria, in the grip of a brutal civil war. Mexican government data released in 2015 showed that between 2007 and 2014, more than 164,000 people were victims of homicide. Many more have been killed since then. Not all homicides are drug or cartel related, but a significant number are organized-crime-style killings.

In what is known as the Northern Triangle in Central America, comprising El Salvador, Honduras, and Guatemala, homicide rates are worse than Europe in the Middle Ages: El Salvador is at 81 homicides, Guatemala at 31, and Honduras at 59 per 100,000. There are all sorts of factors contributing to the breakdown of civil society in these countries—endemic corruption; agrarian conflicts; decades-long civil war (in the case of El Salvador and Guatemala), in which torture and massacre were widespread; deep, intergenerational trauma; the persecution of indigenous peoples; and huge economic and social disparities.

Low homicide rates in the affluent world are often touted as proof that overall levels of violence have declined. That, however, very much depends on who you are and where you live. The high levels of violence in some American cities such as Detroit, New Orleans, Baltimore, and St Louis—ranging from 45 to 60 per 100,000— which are comparable to the high levels of homicide in some Latin American and African cities should cause us to reflect on the impact of violence in different parts of the world. Hyper-masculinity and a desire for respect from one's peers, a lack of confidence in state institutional structures, dysfunctional communities, and an apparent tolerance for violence and a willingness to use it to resolve problems all help explain why some parts of the world are more violent than others.

# Chapter 4
# The sacred and the secular

The state monopolization of violence gained momentum from the 16th century onwards. States declared war on each other, controlled the judicial institutions that meted out violence, decided what constituted a violation of the law, and forcefully constrained their people, through the threat of violence or indeed through the actual physical punishment of lawbreakers, to abide by those laws. It could be argued that, in Europe at least, the emerging sovereign state of the late medieval and early modern period turned to capital punishment as a means of asserting its dominance and the legitimacy of its claim to the monopolization of violence. That is one way of looking at it, but it doesn't really explain the spectacular nature of the violence enacted and performed by the state. It is true that the worst punishments in western Europe were reserved for those who had been found guilty of high treason, petty treason, heresy, and sedition. It was intended, through ritual, symbolism, and ceremony, to convey a wider message—to display the 'natural authority' of the state. According to historian Randall McGowen (following Foucault), this in part stemmed from a lack of means of policing society, but also from a belief that deterrence by terror worked.

The willingness of societies to inflict death on those who deviate from the rules, and the apparent readiness of crowds to enjoy the spectacle of pain and humiliation when it was meted out to people they thought deserved it, are common to all cultures from the ancient world to the modern era. This phenomenon is about the relationship between power and violence. To understand that relationship, I will examine three elements at play: the evolution of the criminal justice system (which varied enormously); changing attitudes towards public executions and torture (why they were less frequently used over time, why executions eventually became hidden from the public); and the role of the state in the use of public executions.

There is an important question fundamental to understanding what is public in these punishments—why did people go and watch what on the surface appears to be such a cruel spectacle? What drove Londoners to hangings, Parisians to someone being drawn and quartered (the method varied, but after being hanged, the victim, still alive, was cut open and the intestines removed and burned—the meaning of drawn; after decapitation, the body was then cut into four parts or sometimes torn apart by four horses— the meaning of quartered), Chinese citizens to a beheading or the act of *lingchi* (death by a thousand cuts), or Americans to someone being lynched? Underlying this question is one that is more complex. Do people across all cultures and across all times share a fundamental psychological make-up that allows us to enjoy the suffering of others? Each period will have its own historically specific reasons for the spectacle of violence but this, it would seem, only tells part of the story. The fact that spectacular violence can be found throughout history—including, one might argue, in the cinema and video games of today—tells us something about human nature and the extent to which violence can be repulsive and yet entertaining and exciting at the same time.

## Torture

The spectacle of the publicly tormented body was part and parcel of social life in Europe, at least before the French Revolution. European legal codes were inspired by ancient Roman traditions, which relied on torture for evidence. In France, there were two kinds of torture: 'preparatory torture', which took place in judicial chambers and which was designed to extract confessions; and 'preliminary torture', which took place in public on the body of the convicted criminal and which was designed to either extract confessions or simply punish the convicted body. Either way, there was a deep-seated belief in the interrelatedness of body, pain, and truth.

This is supposed to have shifted in the 18th century, when attitudes towards pain, death, violence, and suffering changed. At least that was the commonly held view until recently, largely influenced by Foucault's 1975 book, *Discipline and Punish*. It's true that between 1750 and 1850 imprisonment replaced most other punishments, as Foucault states, but there is a debate about whether this was due to the Enlightenment or to earlier changes in the criminal justice system, brought about by legal reforms. Both torture and rates of execution were already declining in Europe during the 17th century, a period during which the utility of corporal punishment began to be called into question and states developed other more effective forms of social control. But to attribute that decline to the Enlightenment is mistaken. The last use of judicial torture in England, for example, occurred in 1640. An exception seems to have been France where, although torture largely fell into neglect, it was still practised on occasion until it was officially abolished by the monarchy in 1788. The French revolutionaries felt the need to abolish it again in 1791, not because it was considered an atrocity, but because it was inextricably linked with the 'social assumptions of absolutism'.

The formal abolition of torture did not mean that it vanished altogether. It continued to be used in Europe's colonies throughout the 19th and 20th centuries, but its use was very different. During the wars of decolonization in the second half of the 20th century, thousands of freedom fighters were tortured by their imperial overlords in Vietnam and Kenya, for example. In

Algeria, French forces tortured, killed, and 'disappeared' thousands of people (a euphemism for killing political prisoners without telling relatives of their fate or the location of their bodies). Torture was a technique used in authoritarian regimes—Stalin's Russia, Hitler's Germany, Mao's China, Pol Pot's Cambodia—as an interrogation technique, as a means of humiliating and degrading prisoners, and as a means of intimidating the population. During the Cold War era, military regimes—Argentina, Chile, Uruguay, and Brazil were the most notorious in South America—kidnapped, detained, and tortured people they considered to be political subversives and then often made them disappear. In Argentina, children were tortured in front of their parents. In Brazil, the military used what was called a 'parrot perch', an iron bar from which a prisoner was hung upside down by his legs and arms, while being beaten or given electric shocks. No one knows how many people were tortured by these Latin American military regimes, but the estimates vary from between 100,000 and 150,000 people. In Uruguay, the worst of the military regimes, it is believed that one in every 50 citizens was interrogated by torture. Our knowledge of torture in Africa is less complete although it was systematically practised in Idi Amin's Uganda and in Robert Mugabe's Zimbabwe. In South Africa under apartheid, the security forces tortured and even burned political prisoners over open fires. Sexualized torture, especially of men, is under-reported.

Of course, it doesn't really make a difference whether torture is legal or not; if the state deems it necessary, it will use it. Despite a 1987 United Nations Convention Against Torture, which has been ratified by 130 countries, torture, or at least the 'cruel, inhuman or degrading treatment' covered by the Convention, is still practised in 141 countries around the world, including by countries that champion democracy, such as the United States and Britain. Some have even tried to justify its use with the theory of 'just torture', used by western powers after 9/11, when it was touted as an acceptable and 'credible' form of extracting confessions, on the pretext of saving 'thousands of lives' in a ticking time-bomb situation. It was an imagined Hollywood-style scenario that never, as far as we know, occurred. The resurgence of state-directed torture in the so-called 'war on terror' is a reversion to what was once unacceptable. Western democratic states are now claiming the right to do what they want to their enemies. One wonders to what extent torturers have been influenced by what they were seeing on TV every day. Between 1995 and 1999, there were 12 scenes of fictional torture on primetime TV. Between 2002 and 2007, that number had increased to 897. Human rights advocacy groups in the United States claim that American interrogators in Iraq were taking their cues from television. In what has become an iconic photo of torture at Abu Ghraib and the invasion of Iraq (Figure 2), a hooded man was forced to stand on a box, wires on his hands and around his neck. He was reportedly told he would be electrocuted if he fell off. The picture is one of many taken by the guards themselves, often smiling for the camera, torturers pleased with their own work.

Torture invariably produces what is now recognized to be Post Traumatic Stress Disorder in the victim both for having survived the horrors of the atrocities committed on his or her body, and for the shame at having spoken against family and friends. But it can also affect the perpetrator or the war criminal, or at least some of them, who must live with the memory and consequences of having committed those atrocities. One can admittedly question a diagnosis that falls on both the victim and the perpetrator. To what extent are German and Japanese perpetrators victims of the Nazi and Imperial states under which they lived? To what extent are American perpetrators in South Vietnam victims of an American imperial policy?

## Capital punishment and the spectacle of violence

Public executions were probably more common than public torture. Hundreds of years before the Roman arena, public

2. The west bringing democracy to Iraq: a hooded man forced to stand on a box in Abu Ghraib.

executions were conducted in town squares. In Ancient Rome, criminals were executed at midday in the arena. One of the more common modes of execution was exposure to wild beasts. Alternatively, prisoners would be burned alive, forced to engage in gladiatorial combats, or simply butchered. After the fall of the

Roman Empire, and up until about the 15th century, executions in Europe were rare and conspicuously unspectacular. For most of the medieval period, crimes against property were treated much more harshly than violent crimes against people, which were often negotiated and resolved by a monetary payment—usually involving both a fine to a legal authority, and a payment to the victim or (in the event of murder) to the victim's family. Over the centuries, however, public executions became increasingly spectacular, reaching a peak in western Europe during the 17th century, followed by a rapid decline. There is then a resurgence during the 18th century. In fact, more people were executed during the 18th and early 19th centuries than in previous centuries.

Some of the punishments reserved for severe crimes—parricide or treason—were horrendous, such as being broken on (or with) the wheel. The executioner broke the prisoner's limbs (either with a wheel or on the wheel, the custom varied) and then set the body on a pole for public viewing. This custom was practised in France until 1787 and in Germany into the 1840s. In Britain during the 18th century, the English Parliament increased the number of crimes punishable by death fivefold, from about 50 in 1688 to about 240 in 1820. In France, by contrast, only six offences incurred capital punishment. Of course, many Britons were able to avoid execution by having their sentences commuted to transportation so that the number of public hangings between 1770 and 1830 declined to a 'relatively modest' 7,000. That changed by the 1840s, when capital offences were essentially reduced to four—high treason, murder, piracy, and the destruction of public arsenals and dockyards.

In London, levels of execution appear to have been connected to moral panics about crime. In the first few decades of the 19th century, executions were taking place more often than any time since the Stuarts. During the course of the 18th century, and across most of western Europe, people began to reflect on ways to exclude violence and force. Public executions were still accepted and were still watched, but sudden death—hanging by what was called the 'drop', or the guillotine—was preferred to the long, drawn-out torment that accompanied hanging by slow strangulation or the act of drawing and quartering. The 'drop' was introduced in London in 1783 as a more effective and more humane form of execution, although 'expense' prevented its regular use in the rest of the country until the first half of the 19th century. Women accused of 'petty treason'—the murder of a spouse—were burned at the stake, although they were commonly strangled beforehand. The last burning of a woman in England took place in 1789; the practice was abandoned the following year. The guillotine, introduced by the French revolutionaries in 1792 as a much more rational, efficient, and humane form of killing, was meant to show just how enlightened the French revolutionaries were. Death was meant to be functional, rather than spectacular. To paraphrase human geographer Marcus A. Doel, violence was no longer made to speak; it was set to work.

For most scholars, the late 18th and early 19th century (in western Europe at least) appears to have been a turning point in attitudes towards pain and suffering, death, and violence. There is general agreement that attitudes changed, but disagreement over the nature of the changes and the reasons why they occurred. The spectacular displays of violence, especially when public executions were involved, appear to have reached a climax between 1400 and 1600. After that, there were still extraordinary displays of state violence and cruelty, but cases began to wane. Norbert Elias, in part influenced by Freud, argued that western Europe underwent a 'civilizing process', which paralleled the monopolization of violence by the absolutist and national states, in which aggressive impulses were tamed or repressed.

That's one way of looking at it, but the timing of and the reasons for the decline are almost impossible to discern. Scholars point to things like the advent of the Enlightenment, the rise of a public sphere, the changes taking place in western economies, and the increasing centralization of the state and its control over people's lives. Reform, when it came, came from above: fear of the mob at a time of revolutionary upheaval, as well as concerns about the immorality of the crowd; the belief that the condemned were not displaying the accepted amount of contrition; the increasing distaste for the smell and sight of mutilated and decomposing bodies put on display after executions; the humanitarian impulse, for want of a better term, emanating from Enlightenment thought; as well as changing views about the privacy of death, all contributed towards changes in attitudes and the law.

Nevertheless, executions were very often major public events paid for by the state and attended by hundreds and, in larger cities, thousands of spectators. In London in the 18th century, up to 100,000 people might turn out to a hanging. It was the behaviour of the crowd along the processional route in London from Newgate prison to Tyburn, near today's Marble Arch, the traditional site of public executions, that was particularly concerning; the civil authorities feared that they had lost control of the process. It was one of the reasons why, in 1783, public hangings were relocated to the front of Newgate prison, although the reasons why this occurred are contested (historian V. A. C. Gatrell argues that this had less to do with humanitarian reasons and more to do with the concerns of property developers). It was nevertheless hoped that by removing the processional aspect of the hanging, and by containing the size of the crowd, public order would be restored. That was not to be. Crowds in the tens of thousands would still regularly turn out to watch hangings, right up to 1868 when public executions were finally banned, but not without a heated debate about the benefits of public hanging.

Judicial killings decreased during the 19th and 20th centuries so that they eventually became scarce and had disappeared altogether in many parts of the world by the second half of the 20th century. Eventually, technology would have a role to play in the execution of the criminal, again with the aim of being more humane. In the United States, the Electrical Execution Act came into force in 1889, despite opposition from an emerging electricity industry. William Kemmler was convicted of murdering his common-law wife, Matilda Ziegler, and was the first person to be executed by electric chair in Auburn, New York, on 6 August 1890. It did not go well; it took more than two minutes to kill the man, who by all accounts died in agony. The last public execution took place in England in 1867, and in France in 1939. In the United States, executions have taken place behind prison walls since 1936 but, depending on state laws, witnesses (such as relatives of the victim and relatives of the prisoner) can still watch an execution.

At the time of writing, capital punishment is still practised in 56 countries around the world, including China, Iran, Saudi Arabia, Iraq, and Egypt. China has by far the highest number of executions each year (it's estimated that 657 people were executed in China in 2019, although Amnesty International believes the real number to be in the thousands). In Japan, the process of execution is surrounded in secrecy: the place of execution is unknown, the prisoner is only informed the morning of the execution, which is held in the middle of the night, and the family of the prisoner often only learns of the execution after the fact through the media.

The decline in capital punishment in the western world over the past two centuries is meant to parallel the rise of a humanitarian discourse. Today, most western nations have abolished capital punishment, but over 60 per cent of the world's population live in countries where the death penalty is retained. In those countries, debates over the abolition of capital punishment, if they occur, often centre on the sanctity of human life.

## Religion and violence

The Enlightenment and the French Revolution were in part about separating religion from the state. Enlightenment philosophers were convinced that peace would only come to the earth when monarchy and religion were abolished, or as the French *philosophe*, Denis Diderot, put it, 'Man will never be free until the last king is strangled with the entrails of the last priest.' The sentiment foreshadows the revolutionary violence that would later descend on France, but this division between the church and the state, between the spiritual and the secular, did not exist for most of human history. It would have been unthinkable for anyone who lived on this planet before the modern era to separate religion from politics or from everyday life, and there are still many parts of the world where religion and politics are inseparable. The extent to which religion may have caused or incited violence in the past is nevertheless a rich area for debate. Much depends on how you define religion and its influence.

On the one hand there are prominent atheist intellectuals like Richard Dawkins, Christopher Hitchens, and Sam Harris for whom the very nature of religion leads to violence. William Cavanagh and Karen Armstrong, on the other hand, argue against these claims. Armstrong argues that modern societies have made a scapegoat of faith, and that large-scale organized violence is not linked with religion, but with both human nature and the state. In a 2004 historical audit undertaken by the BBC of all the major conflicts over the past 3,500 years, wars were ranked between 0 and 5 according to the extent to which they were religious, motivated by religion, or led by leaders who were religious. The Peloponnesian Wars (around 460 BCE) ranked 0 (not religious) while the Crusades ranked 5 (very religious). Al-Qaeda ranked 4 while the invasion of Iraq in 2004 ranked 3 (largely because George W. Bush stated that God was on his side). Most wars over the last 3,500 years were ranked 0 or 1. In other words, the conclusion of this audit was that there were few wars that were truly religious in nature.

The audit is one way of looking at the question, but it doesn't consider religious 'movements' throughout history that have led to untold deaths, such as the pursuit of heretics and witches in

Europe, or the Taiping rebellion in China, which cost the lives of millions of people. The existence of violent cults is also missing; think of the apocalyptic cult in Jonestown, Guyana, where 900 people committed suicide, and the siege in Waco, Texas, that killed 86 people. Nor does it consider the religious inflections in social and political upheavals, as well as in warfare, that have gone on through the ages. Finally, it does not tell us whether religion causes more violence or whether it is a pathway towards a more peaceful world or society. I would argue that religion is both. Religion has the potential to be tolerant and accepting, and to be utterly intolerant and unaccepting, verging on the genocidal. Everything depends on the historical and cultural context.

Much of the religious violence in the past was highly ritualized, from human sacrifice to ceremonial cannibalism to scalping in certain North American and Mesoamerican peoples. In these instances, violence was spiritual, but demonstrating a causal link between violence and religion is more problematic. In the modern west, religion is no longer as central to society as it once was, but it is still a powerful force in many other parts of the world. One of the more pressing issues of our century is the outbreak of extremist violence and terrorism, often in the name of religion. It would appear, for example, that Sunni–Shi'a tensions in the Middle East that have led to thousands of deaths are religiously motivated, although the line between politics and religion is often blurred. When religion is a factor in violent extremism—always a debatable point—perhaps the best way of approaching the question is to look at it as part of a larger culture of violence among communities that believe they are under attack. Messianic Zionists, militant Christians, Indian Sikhs, Buddhists, and Muslim fundamentalists can all commit acts of violence in the name of their religion. Moreover, religion can still play a role in violence and warfare in the modern era by offering an 'alternative reality' that provides believers with an ideological framework that can feed into violence. Religion is not necessarily the cause of violence, but it often offers a moral justification.

# Chapter 5
# Collective and communal violence

In contrast to interpersonal or intimate violence, which often involves violent encounters between individuals or small groups of people, collective violence can involve crowds of people, sometimes referred to pejoratively as the mob, as well as groups that are part of a specific organization (more or less organized depending on the circumstances). Different kinds of collective violence have existed throughout history, from subsistence riots and large-scale revolts to revolutions. Much of the collective unrest in Europe, China, and India over the centuries was subsistence related, that is, there were long traditions of food riots and tax revolts brought about by the fear of starvation. Riots around food supplies or food shortages had largely ceased in Europe by the middle of the 19th century as greater agricultural productivity, modern transportation, and an increasingly urbanized landscape finally solved the problems of supply that had once provoked local outbursts in the western world. Instances of collective violence centred around food supply are now largely a thing of the past, even if there are sporadic eruptions, such as those we saw in Africa and Bengal in 2007–8, when worldwide commodity prices rose sharply, and in Venezuela in 2016–17, when he disastrous economic situation resulted in thousands of protests.

There are two distinctions to be made here: what might be called spontaneous collective action, occasions during which people react to what they see as an injustice; and prolonged, large-scale collective action, which requires an organization of some kind to take the lead. I'll look at the distinction between these two forms of violence in a moment, but collective violence can also range from the criminal to the political, from gangs and organized crime to riots, to strikes and social movements that might turn violent if they see no other way to achieve their goals. We have seen this in any number of movements in the first decades of the 21st century, including clashes between white extremists and antifa (the antifascists movement), as well as the Black Lives Matter movement, and the pro-democracy movement in Hong Kong in 2019–20.

It is not possible to cover adequately every kind of collective violence here or to make any overarching conclusions. I will, however, focus on four different types of collective violence and how they may have evolved over the centuries. The first two entail revolt and revolution; what motivates people to riot and revolt (other than food), what drives them, on occasion, to commit acts of atrocity against figures of authority, and behave in a crowd in ways they would never consider doing as individuals, and what drives communities to overthrow governments? The third consists of religious and ethnic (or race) riots (the two were often but not always intertwined), which continued in Europe well into the 20th century, and which continue to take place in other parts of the world today. Two case studies will help illustrate this: the pogrom in eastern Europe; and lynching in the United States. The fourth form of collective violence is the criminal. I'll look at gang-related violence in the Americas. Let me begin, however, by looking at the vexed question of a 'crowd mentality'.

## The crowd mentality

Is there such a thing as a crowd mentality that allows people to commit acts of violence in group settings they would never consider doing as individuals? The classic text on the crowd is a book by Gustave le Bon written in 1895. Called *The Crowd: A Study of the Popular Mind*, it was translated into sixteen languages and became one of the most influential psychology texts of all time. It not only theorized but created the idea of mass politics in the 20th century and was cited by Mussolini and Goebbels. Le Bon argues that when people get together in a crowd, they lose their individuality. Because individuality is the basis of judgement and reason, people become subject to *contagion* in a crowd, unable to resist any passing idea or emotion. People subsequently regress to something more primitive, something more brutal. The crowd then is irrational, and it can be violent. Le Bon writes:

> … by the mere fact that he forms part of an organized crowd, a man descends several rungs in the ladder of civilization. Isolated, he may be a cultivated individual; in a crowd, he is a barbarian—that is, a creature acting by instinct.…An individual in a crowd is a grain of sand amid other grains of sand, which the wind stirs up at will.

This view is, however, political, and is therefore a defence of the status quo; it is aimed at proving the 'common people' should be feared as a potential threat to civilization. Most crowds are not violent (consider concerts, most sporting events, and most demonstrations). Many sociologists, psychologists, and social scientists today do not accept the idea of a 'crowd mentality'. Stephen Reicher, who challenges the pathologizing of crowds, argues that people do not surrender their identity or lose themselves in the group. Instead, individuals who join the group embrace a collective identity, one usually framed by rules. This is certainly the case for football hooligans in Europe, who are often highly organized and follow ritualistic patterns of violence. Crowds are not entities that exist outside of a specific social context. They are responses to specific events and shaped (and limited) by the concerns of those who form the crowd.

Three other, more recent sociological theories address crowd behaviour. The first is Convergence Theory, whose proponents argue that the behaviour of a crowd is the result of like-minded individuals with pre-existing values and beliefs coming together. If the crowd becomes violent it is because the people who came together in the crowd wanted it to be violent. Then there is Emergent Norm Theory, whose proponents argue that behaviours are only determined after like-minded individuals come together, and that they are largely rational. One of the more influential theories—Value-Added Theory (also called Structural-Strain Theory)—argues that social movements and other collective behaviours only occur if four preconditions are met: *structural strain*, when people are angry and frustrated by societal problems; *generalized beliefs*, which include both people's understanding of societal problems and their solutions for resolving them; *precipitating factors*, events that suddenly spark a riot/movement/ demonstration; and *lack of social control* when participants do not expect to be arrested or otherwise punished. All these conditions must exist for any kind of collective behaviour to occur. The storming of the Capitol building in Washington by an angry mob in January 2021 appears to be an example.

## The crowd and the 'culture of retribution'

As with food riots, collective political disturbances appear to have become less frequent in Europe over time. Summarizing the long-term trends, the American sociologist Charles Tilly stated that:

> On the whole, the repertoires of contention that began to prevail in Western Europe and North America during the nineteenth century had lower probabilities of producing violence than their predecessors. Not only shaming ceremonies, but also invasions of posted fields, seizures of grain, expulsions of unwelcome representatives of authority, machine-breaking, destruction of dishonoured houses, and a number of other forms of direct action were well-known

violence producing routines in the eighteenth century that almost disappeared during the nineteenth.

Tilly found, for example, that in 18th- and early 19th-century England, the number of meetings, riots, demonstrations, and assemblies had not necessarily declined, but the percentage of gatherings at which people were killed or injured dropped sharply. In other words, political contestation was becoming less violent. There were exceptions to this rule, such as the Peterloo Massacre of 16 August 1819, when militia attacked protesters in Manchester demanding parliamentary reform; the attack led to 18 killed and hundreds injured. Before that, the Gordon Riot of 1780, brought about by an attempt to reduce discrimination against Catholics, was the most violent and prolonged unrest in 18th-century England with 285 dead and 200 wounded.

Throughout most of European history, riots and revolts (urban and rural) rejected change, whether it was economic, political, or religious. And they occurred frequently. According to one study conducted by a group of French researchers led by Jean Nicolas, more than 8,500 incidents in which four or more people were involved took place in France alone between 1661 and 1789. The French historian Aurélien Lignereux has inventoried a total of 460 revolts between 1800 and 1813, in the territories annexed to the French Empire. Another 71 revolts can be added for the year 1814. And that is not counting the 1,000 or so revolts that took place inside France. Historians tend to focus on violent unrest, but that can skew our perspective. As a recent work has shown for the French Revolution, the majority of protests in the streets of Paris between 1787 and 1795 were non-violent. It would be interesting to see whether this was the case for urban environments elsewhere in Europe and beyond, or the extent to which French popular politics may have influenced protests in other parts of the world.

Violence, then, was not the first response but was often the culmination of an array of responses to what was perceived as an injustice—a new tax or an increase in taxation, the price of grain and of bread, the mandatory billeting of soldiers, a change in systems of agriculture—or by a new incursion of the state or local authority. There was no such thing as a typical riot and most had several causes. In England, the biggest cause of popular protest in the 16th and 17th centuries was the enclosure of common lands. Protests were characterized for the most part by an attack on authority figures for what were perceived to be abuses of power. This is what the historian William Beik calls an expression of the 'culture of retribution'. That is, there was an element of vengeance in crowd behaviour bent on punishing people who should have known better.

According to some scholars, the nature of collective violence in Europe changed over time. If Charles Tilly believed that they were becoming less lethal, William Beik's views are more ambivalent. He argues that the violence carried out by the crowds had its roots in traditional revolts and riots that had been practised for centuries. The crowds had always attacked people in authority if they thought they were abusing their power. However, the traditional patterns of violence—'retributive violence'—changed over time, and the French Revolution seems to mark a turning point. During the Revolution, and possibly for the first time, we begin to see decapitated heads being paraded around on pikes as trophies. Of course, the decapitated heads and the remains of convicts had often been displayed on castle walls and raven-stones (a raised platform on which the corpse of the executed was left; the name is a reference to the birds that came to feast on the rotting body) in the medieval and early modern period, while body parts had been displayed and even sold during the French Wars of Religion (1562–98), as a means of humiliating the victim. But the violence of the revolutionary crowd, according to Beik, was the result of a new kind of emotion—joy mixed with fear.

The Revolution saw the invention of a new ritual language that quickly spread—and died out almost as quickly—within a few years. Let's look at one example. In September 1792, news reached Paris that a Prussian army had invaded France and was advancing towards the capital. At the same time, rumours circulated that Parisians who secretly opposed the Revolution would help prepare for their arrival. Radicals, known as Jacobins, broke into the prisons where they began to kill the prisoners—priests, nobles, women, common law prisoners—because they were feared to be counter-revolutionaries. Between 1,100 and 1,400 prisoners were killed in a matter of days.

There is here a fundamental shift in collective violence, from wanting to punish and humiliate those held responsible for injustices and wrongs, to wanting to physically eliminate those seen to be political enemies. But a further change took place during the Revolution so that the state, once again, assumed control of violence. Popular violence gave way to revolutionary state violence. I'll come back to state violence in the next chapter, but during the Terror of 1793–4, there is both the execution of around 40,000 people across all classes (nobles, clergy, peasants, workers) considered counter-revolutionaries, as well as the horror of civil war in the region known as the Vendée in the west of France that may have claimed up to 250,000 insurgent and 200,000 Republican lives.

## Revolutions

Revolutions have occurred wherever there have been highly complex, stratified societies, although they are generally rare events. The word itself was first used in the 16th century, in Renaissance Italy—*revolutio*—to describe the frequent changes in power taking place. It was only in the modern era that it came to mean a fundamental break with the past, usually through the violent overthrow of the existing regime. The major revolutions of the modern era were extraordinarily complex events, and have been the object of intense study, heated debate, and much theorizing, so it is impossible here to sum up the reasons why each of these revolutions descended into greater or lesser degrees of violence.

What distinguishes a simple revolt or a large riot from a revolution? The answer is an idea, coupled with a desire for radical social and political change. At the same time, a revolution is guided but not necessarily brought about by an organizing principle, an ideology whose goal is the complete renewal of society. That ideology can be promoted by an organization that has adopted it as its guiding principle. That was the case, for example, for the Bolsheviks in Russia. In many of the major revolutions that have occurred since the end of the 18th century, once a revolution begins, violence often becomes an integral part of the process, including political and social purges as the revolution swings from moderate to radical, and as society and the polity are completely transformed. This often results in civil war, as well as war with other states, sometimes because revolutionaries embark on a crusade to bring their ideology to others, but also because other groups or states intervene to restore the old order. In the case of anti-colonial revolutions, what are also dubbed 'wars of decolonization', they too can spread to neighbouring countries. This happened with the American, French, Haitian, Mexican, Russian, and Chinese Revolutions, but also with Latin America and Vietnam.

Revolutionaries tend to be zealots who see the world in unequivocal terms, that is, one is either for or against their ideology and cause. The consequence of this is that anyone who opposes the prevailing ideology is considered an obstacle to the fulfilment of revolutionary goals; they become enemies and are destined to be persecuted and often eliminated. That is often done with brutal and ruthless efficiency. As a result, revolutionary leaders will appear, only to be destroyed later by their own as the process becomes more radical and more authoritarian. This happened to Danton and Robespierre during the French Revolution, and to people like Trotsky, Zinoviev, and Bukharin during the Russian Revolution. It was, in fact, a pattern that has repeated itself in just about every modern revolution, from North Korea and Vietnam to Iran. This dynamic has led at least one revolutionary group to see the external world as morally corrupt, as was the case with Pol Pot and the Khmer Rouge in Cambodia. Pol Pot attempted to wipe the slate clean, sweeping aside all existing political and social structures, and to start again, with the devastating consequences known as the 'killing fields', in which more than one million people were killed by the Khmer Rouge regime from 1975 to 1979.

Why revolutions occur are as varied as the revolutions themselves, although it is possible to identify common patterns. There are, always, a number of structural factors that can come into play, including the disaffection of elites with the regime, and serious economic and fiscal crises that bring states to the brink of bankruptcy, often on the back of rising costs of living and food shortages. Fiscal and economic crises can be exacerbated by major natural disasters, as happened with the French Revolution, or they can come on the heels of serious military setbacks, as happened with the Russian Revolution. All these things can undermine the authority and legitimacy of the state (or the head of state), but they must also occur at a time when there is general and mounting popular disaffection, and when the coercive institutions of the state (such as the army or the police) begin to waver and side with the protesters. Once rulers have completely lost touch with the bulk of the population and continue to pursue policies that alienate elites and the people from the state even further, the regime comes to be seen as illegitimate and unjust. This happened in Ceaușescu's Romania in 1989.

Despite these characteristics, not all revolutions are violent, and not all revolutions enter what might be called a radical phase. This is what happened with the so-called Velvet Revolution in Czechoslovakia in 1989, as well as the Colour Revolutions of the early 2000s. In these instances, there was no elite disaffection, the state was in control of its coercive forces, and the governments relatively stable. These were movements that overthrew corrupt regimes but were often in turn replaced by corrupt regimes with authoritarian tendencies. This occurred in Ukraine and during the Arab Spring and in eastern Europe today.

What of the legacies of revolutions? The results are mixed to say the least. The American Revolution was meant to institute a democratic regime, and it did up to a point, but it also created a polity based on slavery that led to political secession and civil war in 1860. The French Revolution resulted in a bitter civil war and 1 million dead, and 22 years of warfare that resulted in millions dying across Europe. The Russian Revolution also resulted in millions of deaths in civil war, and eventually in a regime under Stalin whose collectivization, mass deportations, and political repression caused millions more deaths. Similarly, the Chinese civil war, and the Cultural Revolution that followed, occasioned several million deaths. Revolutions, in short, do not often lead to increased freedoms and human rights. In fact, several 20th-century revolutions have led to curtailed freedoms and the introduction of authoritarian regimes that are often far worse than those that preceded them.

## Race and religion in collective violence

Other types of collective violence are intertwined with ethnicity and religion. This is the case, for example, for riots between Muslims and Hindus and between Hindus and Sikhs in India, as well as Buddhist attacks on Muslims in Myanmar. Let's focus on pogroms against Jews in Europe, which occurred for nine centuries right up until the end of the Second World War. The word 'pogrom' can be traced to the Russian for 'thunder' or 'storm', but it was first used to refer to outbreaks of anti-Jewish violence by non-Jewish street mobs in the Russian Empire from 1881 to 1884. It has since become a byword for rioting regardless of time or place. Most of the original pogroms took place in an area that became known as the Pale of Settlement, a territory acquired by the Russian Empire between 1791 and 1835 (which included present-day Belarus, Lithuania, and Moldova, much of Ukraine and Poland, and some parts of Latvia and Russia). The Russian government forbade its Jewish subjects from settling in Russian territory outside the Pale of Settlement. Although an 1821 attack in Odessa is sometimes considered to be the first pogrom in the Russian Empire, most historians cite the 1881 incidents beginning in Elizavetgrad (in present-day Ukraine) as the beginning of the Russian pogrom phenomenon. The Elizavetgrad violence spread rapidly throughout seven provinces in southern Russia and Ukraine, where peasant attackers looted Jewish stores and homes, and destroyed property. Many individuals were beaten and/or murdered and women raped in these pogroms. In 1881, pogroms also occurred in Kiev and Odessa among a hundred other locations. The main inspiration for these vicious attacks was the ideology of anti-Semitism; Jews were blamed for everything from weakened economic conditions to political instability. In addition, there was the claim that Jews murdered Jesus, and the myth of blood libel that charged Jews with murdering Christian babies and baking their blood into *matzah* (a Jewish flatbread used in Passover).

Pogroms continued to occur into the early 20th century, sometimes fomented by Russian officials (Figure 3). Particularly violent were the pogroms from 1903 to 1906. The horrific 1903 pogrom in Kishinev, in what is now Moldova, killed dozens of Jews and resulted in the destruction of hundreds of homes and businesses, prompting tens of thousands of Russian Jews to flee. Estimates of the number of Jews killed during the Russian civil war (1918–22) range from between 50,000 and 200,000, with many thousands of Jewish girls and women raped. This phenomenon was present in central Europe during the inter-war period and carried over into street violence against Jews in Nazi Germany. On 9–10 November 1938, a wave of violence known as *Kristallnacht* (Night of Broken Glass) was instigated by the Nazi

3. Jews killed in the 1904 Bialystok pogrom are laid down outside the Jewish hospital.

Party. Street violence against Jews continued throughout the Second World War. In many areas under German occupation, Nazi officials and soldiers supported and encouraged pogroms. After the war, pogroms continued in Europe. A pogrom occurred in 1946 in Kielce, Poland, against Jewish Holocaust survivors who returned to the town, leaving 42 dead. These pogroms further motivated the already devastated Jewish population to seek refuge outside Europe.

In America, collective violence was a common feature of life well into the 19th century; riots could be triggered by any number of reasons, but they usually had to do with race, ethnicity, employment, and political affiliations. The city of New York, for example, with a population of fewer than 200,000, experienced more than 70 ethnic, labour, and political riots between 1788 and 1834. Some, such as the New York riot of 1863, involved hundreds of people and lasted days, ending with around 120 people killed and 2,000 wounded. One of the largest race riots in the United

States occurred in 1921 when the prosperous all-black community of Greenwood in Tulsa was destroyed after a black shoeshine boy was charged with assaulting a white elevator girl. No one knows how many people were killed, hundreds probably, but at least 800 were injured. Both of those riots were racial massacres instigated by whites against black communities, but black Americans also rioted, as we saw during the Civil Rights movement of the 1960s and the Los Angeles riot of 1992 in what the historian Elizabeth Hinton has called violent rebellion.

Vigilantism blossomed in frontier regions, especially the west, and continued in the south for a century after the Civil War had come to an end. In some regions of the United States, authorities sometimes sanctioned and even participated in, and invariably turned a blind eye to the violence that served to maintain the institution of white supremacy. Between 1882 and 1968, 4,733 people were lynched in the United States, most, but not all of them, black (Figure 4). About a third were considered 'white' (that is, Italians, Mexicans, and others who were accused, in the language of the time, of being 'nigger lovers'). It is difficult of course to make generalizations, but when dealing with mass killings or lynchings by mobs, the victim is often killed twice, so to speak. After the lynching, the body is mutilated, beaten with whatever is to hand, burned, and dismembered. All these atrocities are about humiliating the victim further, and in the process making them unrecognizable, less than human, but it is also about sending a message to the living.

## Gang violence in the Americas

A more recent contributing factor to collective violence is organized crime perpetrated by gangs. In Central America they are known as *maras*; in the slums of Nairobi they are known as the Mungimki; in Los Angeles, the Eighteenth Street Gang controls parts of their neighbourhood; in Salvador, it's the MS-13. There are many different types of gangs, from low-level street

4. The lynching of teenager Lige Daniels on 3 August 1920, in the small town of Center, Texas.

gangs to large groups that carry out turf wars and are involved in transnational criminal enterprises. People are murdered for any number of gang-related infringements: refusing to join a gang; joining the wrong gang; or refusing to cooperate with a gang when asked to do something, including sometimes handing over property (for example, a house or a farm). They share some traits with perpetrators of massacres, mass killings, and genocide in that the individual members bow to peer group pressure to kill. Gangs adopt honour codes that are like the codes once practised by men in other cultures, in other times, such as in Italy during the Renaissance, or in Greece during the 19th century.

According to the Mexican sociologist Raúl Rodríguez Guillén, there were more public lynchings in Mexico in 2015—at least 78—than at any other time in the last quarter-century (Figure 5). That was more than double the number in 2014. There were another 60 lynching incidents in Mexico in 2017, and 174 in 2018, 58 of which resulted in deaths. Not all the lynchings are carried out by drug cartels. Sometimes, they are the result of mob justice, people who turn on suspected criminals. There are several ways of interpreting lynchings in Central America, including broader

**5. Suspected members of Los Zetas drugs cartel found hanging from a bridge in Nuevo Laredo, Mexico, on 4 May 2012.**

explanations around culture, and the absence of a strong civil society, but let me outline two. The first is to see it as the result of mob actions born of a sense of hopelessness and impotence shared by many. In Mexico, for example, 98 per cent of murders go unsolved, and the state is virtually absent in some areas. By some estimates, just 12 per cent of crimes are even reported in Mexico, largely because of a lack of faith that justice will ever be served. The other way to see it is its exact opposite. Rather than signalling the absence of the state, lynching is an expression of a community's reaction towards a state presence that is perceived as intrusive and illegitimate. The lynchings, according to this theory, imitate the brutality of extra-legal forms of violence perpetrated by public officials at the local level. The reality is quite likely a combination of these two approaches.

The two questions that have often plagued scholars of collective violence are what causes variations in the level and form of violence over time, and how and why do participants fluctuate between peaceful and violent social interactions? As we have seen, the answers to those questions invariably change with the form of collective violence being examined. Certainly, there has been a diminution of subsistence-related unrest around the world, one possible benefit of the modernization of food production. On the other hand, social movements that begin as peaceful social protests can turn violent, but they are overall less violent than in previous centuries. There are exceptions to this rule. At the time of writing, there were more than 700 civilians killed and many hundreds more injured in protests in Myanmar since the coup of 1 February 2021. I would suggest from this brief outline that different forms of collective violence are often interconnected, although we are yet to adequately understand those relationships.

# Chapter 6
# Violence and the state

Some historians, inspired by the German sociologist Max Weber, have argued that as states gained a monopoly over violence, as they became more powerful, more centralized, and more bureaucratic, interpersonal violence declined. In other words, the state took charge of justice and made itself responsible for carrying out the punishment of criminals. By assuming responsibility for the exercise of violence, the state was able to reduce levels of violence among ordinary people. It's a powerful argument, and it makes quite a bit of sense, but it does not present us with an entirely accurate understanding of violence and the state. It is also based on the assumption that any reduction of violence must come from above, and that those who are most directly touched by violence have little or no agency. The role of civil society in controlling levels of violence does not appear to play a part in the Weberian model.

There are other points that are worth making about the role of the state and violence. The first is that the state—which we will define as an organized political community under a government that rules over a defined territory—always reduces levels of violence, but this is not always the case—think of warfare, political purges, and state-sponsored genocides. The state's monopolization of violence and state-sponsored genocides around the world has made it one of, if not *the*, key vectors of violence in the 19th and

20th centuries. It includes the Armenian genocide, collectivization in the Soviet Union which resulted in the Great Famine in which millions died, the Holocaust, and the Cambodian genocide. Think too of the Nazi euthanasia programme, which resulted in the deaths of up to 200,000 people, and the eugenics programme in the United States in the first half of the 20th century that led to over 70,000 women being forcibly sterilized. Then there is the sociologist Mark Cooney's argument that as the state's power increased and as some forms of violence declined, other forms became much more private. That is, violence simply evolved and changed, not just quantitively but also qualitatively.

This chapter will focus on four themes—colonialism, state-sanctioned violence, extreme violence against civilians in warfare, and terrorism. Political violence can take many forms, including extra-legal warfare, ethnic cleansing, civil war, terrorism and state repression, revolution, and counter-revolution. It can also encompass state as well as non-state actors and acts of violence that might be carried out for political, secular, or religious reasons. We also need to make a distinction between violence and warfare, interconnected but different phenomena. I looked at rape in warfare in Chapter 5, so I'll limit my remarks here to the kinds of violence that often accompany organized warfare, such as massacres and atrocities, the role of race, and the increased technological potential to kill larger numbers of people, both combatant and non-combatant. There will be some inevitable and unavoidable overlap, but violence is not something that can be clearly categorized and contained.

## Colonialism, race, and violence

Violence has always been central to the long, complex history of colonialism that stretches back centuries. Colonial violence was diffuse, multi-layered, and varied enormously, but as a rule, as interpersonal violence in Europe declined in the modern era, levels of violence against non-Europeans in the colonies increased.

While violence is far from unique to colonial practices, it was always embedded in the social, legal, economic, and gendered foundations on which colonial relations were built.

A broad distinction can be made between 'exploitative colonialism' and 'settler colonialism'. Exploitative colonialism was predicated on extracting primary resources and labour from colonized territories for the benefit of the imperial centre. This was the case for the British Raj. Settler colonialism was predicated on taking possession of new territories and transporting people from the metropole to the colonies, as well as the exploitation and extraction of resources for the metropole. This was the case for countries like Australia, New Zealand, and regions like Africa, and the Americas. By its very nature, then, colonization involved the subjugation of peoples and their lands, cultures, and laws. The justification was that Europeans were bringing civilization and enlightenment to 'savages' and 'primitive peoples'. The use of pervasive and everyday violence was also justified on the grounds that indigenes were ignorant, but race too had a role to play in this violence. Europeans often looked upon indigenes as vermin. Revolts and rebellions often met with brutal repression. The Mutiny of 1857 in India is a case in point, but there are countless examples from the European and American colonizing experiences in which punitive colonial campaigns, of varying levels of intensity, ruthlessly put down rebellions and unrest.

An array of violent strategies was used by European colonial powers to dominate the rest of the world throughout the latter part of the 19th and into the 20th centuries. Martial law, paramilitary policing, and corporal punishment were extensively used by imperial states to maintain control of indigenous peoples, while settlers carried out massacres on the colonial frontier against local peoples who opposed incursions onto their territory. Indigenous and local peoples in turn resisted, sometimes in haphazard ways. After the Second World War, in what became known as wars of independence (or wars of decolonization) against the European powers, the colonized revolted against the colonizer in national movements throughout Africa and Asia. Most of the violence carried out by colonial powers against the colonized remains unrecorded. Skirmishes, small confrontations, and massacres on the frontier, for example, were often overlooked or simply not reported, and were never considered to be part of ongoing wars against the colonized.

In fact, there have been very few attempts to count the number of clashes that took place across European and American colonial possessions. During Queen Victoria's reign at least 228 known armed conflicts took place across the British Empire from 1837 to 1901, a figure that vastly underestimates the number of small battles and forms of guerrilla warfare that were fought on colonial frontiers. Over the same era, for example, potentially hundreds of skirmishes were fought on the Australian frontier alone, some of them recorded only indirectly and many of them not recorded at all. This code of silence among murdering settlers has a history too. Thus, the squatter Henry Meyrick, writing of Victoria in the 1840s in *Life in the Bush*, noted how Aboriginal people were hunted down. Men, women, and children were 'shot whenever they can be met with. I have protested against it at every station I have been in...in the strongest language, but these things are kept very secret as the penalty would certainly be hanging.'

This code of silence was not peculiar to Australia and had a role to play in settler violence in North America and South Africa. All settler societies seem to have several characteristics in common. First, wherever settler societies encountered indigenous peoples, killing and massacres occurred. In north Africa, and more specifically Algeria, the French military used razzias, a tactic of swift and brutal raids conducted against recalcitrant Algerian communities to repress all resistance. We do not know how many Algerians died in the 19th-century wars of conquest, but scholars have suggested anywhere between 500,000 and 1 million out of an estimated 3 million Algerians. Second, the frequency of colonial reprisals and massacres increased throughout the 19th century with the intensification of the European empires' territorial ambitions. Third, colonial violence often occurred on such a small scale that it could be hidden from metropolitan oversight, but sometimes it occurred on a disturbingly large scale and was openly or implicitly condoned, or sometimes retrospectively condemned by the colonial state. Such was the case for the Amritsar (Jallianwalla Bagh) massacre of 1919, in which the British Indian Army fired upon a crowd of peaceful protesters, resulting in casualties thought to be in the range of 1,000 to 1,500.

Massacres, brute force, the elimination of indigenous peoples, and the repression of resistance to colonial incursions are the most obvious forms of violence used by settlers on the frontier. But, as Patrick Wolfe has famously argued, not all strategies geared towards 'the elimination of the native' required the use of physical force. The European imperial state had a wide array of policies to regulate indigenous peoples, including institutional violence and cultural coercion directed at the 'dissolution' of indigenous societies. These coercive strategies included officially encouraged miscegenation (which authorities around the colonial world believed would lead to the disappearance of indigenous bloodlines); programmes of religious conversion; the removal of indigenous children from their families for placement in missions or training schools; and prohibitions against speaking indigenous languages. These programmes were designed to ultimately absorb indigenous people into the colonial body politic, to assimilate them so that they would eventually become white. The colonial state was also built and managed through a variety of other violent strategies, but here I will focus on four.

First, colonial governors declared martial law throughout the British and French Empires when unruly frontiers could not be brought to order through ordinary legal means. From the mid-19th century with the arrival of colonial self-government, martial law took on more clearly draconian roles to repress insurgency, to control indigenous subjects, or to contain settler demands. In 1865, for example, Jamaica's governor Edward John Eyre used the authority of martial law to put to death 439 indigenous insurgents during the Morant Bay Rebellion. Although this event outraged liberals in the metropole, who attempted to have him convicted of murder on three separate occasions, Eyre was acquitted.

Second, paramilitary police forces, which included the widespread use of 'native' forces, enabled colonial governments to extend their control over resistant indigenous populations in ways that civil policing could not. In this sense, while paramilitary police forces varied in composition across different colonial settings, they shared a fundamental role to build and to protect the economic and political goals of empire. Strategies of colonial policing ranged along a spectrum, as historian Richard Price has pointed out, from the 'benignly hegemonic' to the overtly coercive, but their purpose was always to enforce the laws of the ruling colonial power.

Third, the flogging of indigenous peoples remained a normal aspect of many colonial societies, despite humanitarian reforms over the 19th century that saw its use decline for other subjects of empire. In South Africa, for example, about 4,000 men were sentenced to receive cuts or lashes between 1911 and 1914 alone. Sometimes the recipients of these discretionary punishments were flogged to death, but although such cases produced moral outrage in the metropole, they had little impact in reining in the behaviour of settlers who considered it their right to control their workers as they saw fit. More widely, corporal punishment took some extreme forms. In King Leopold's Congo, for instance, where the line between private and state-sanctioned violence was blurred, the amputation of workers' hands and limbs was practised as a form of punishment on those who did not meet rubber quotas—even young children were not spared. Between 1880 and 1920, around 10 million people were murdered, worked, or starved to death in the Congo. The whole country may have been the personal property of the Belgian king, but the violence was committed at the local level with the complicity of government authorities.

The idea of corporal punishment, and the instilling of terror, was consistent with the notion that severe punishment was integral to reform, that a just measure of pain was necessary to modify criminal behaviour. Salutary terror—violence intended to condition 'good behaviour' in indigenous peoples—was the point at which state violence legitimized settler violence. It normalized coercion as a necessary part of the pacifying, 'civilizing process'. Whether authorized by colonial states or committed covertly, violence had become such an extensive strategy of conquest by the late 19th and early 20th centuries that scholars have linked the colonial project to the elimination of indigenous peoples. This line of enquiry has also produced some controversial debates about the purported genocidal nature of colonialism and its links to the Nazi Holocaust.

Finally, hunger was also used as a tactic to control local populations. There were three famine periods—1876–8, 1896–7, and again in 1899–1902—that affected different parts of the world, including India and China, but also Korea, Vietnam, the Philippines, and Brazil, regions where minimal human-subsistence diets were introduced by colonial authorities and which, as a result, led to the deaths of anywhere between 32 and 61 million people. In southern Tanzania in the 1890s, the German military systematically destroyed fields and granaries. The tactical use of hunger to control local populations was, according to some historians, the result of Malthusian economic policies, the idea that population always outgrows food supplies so that populations need to be controlled. Hunger was also a strategy imported back to Europe, used during the First World War when the Allies blockaded Germany to starve the population. The blockade continued after the guns had fallen silent, to pressure Germany to sign a treaty, so that at least 400,000 Germans starved to death in 1918. We have also seen the Soviet and Chinese Communist states practising hunger as a means of controlling or eliminating sections of their own populations with enormously devastating consequences.

## The concentration camp

This leads us to a discussion about the links between colonialism and the concentration camp. After all, the concentration camp emerged not in Europe, but among European powers incarcerating locals in the colonies. An argument could be made that the modern concentration camp had its predecessor in state-run camps for indigenous peoples in North America and Australia in the 19th century. The conditions in these proto-camps were similar to the modern concentration camp: disease, malnutrition, exposure to the elements, and unsanitary conditions led to high mortality rates. Governments often deliberately withheld support or allowed mismanagement in the hope that the indigenous populations would die. In late 19th-century colonial wars, the modern camp as we understand it emerged when locals were deliberately isolated so as not to lend support to anti-colonial or guerrilla movements. This was a tactic adopted by the Spanish in the Cuban War of Independence (1895–8), the Americans in the Philippines (1899–1902), the British during the Boer War (1899–1902, along with the widespread use of a product originally meant for farming called barbed wire), and the Germans in south-west Africa (1904–8). In each case, tens of thousands of civilians died from disease and malnutrition. Given the time frame, it is worth asking whether European powers learned from one another or whether the practices specific to the camps—torture, forced labour, hunger—emerged independently at the same time in different regions of the globe. The answer to that question is complicated by the fact that there is no typical concentration camp. The nature and purpose of the camp can vary enormously, from the British 'concentration camps' in South Africa through to the Soviet gulag, the German system of *Konzentrationslager* in occupied Europe, or the internment of Japanese in the United

States during the Second World War. They are all camps but they each had a different purpose.

The use of camps expanded dramatically during the First World War. Millions of citizens—enemy aliens as well as nationals who had been stripped of their citizenship—were interned, as were millions of POWs, often in conditions that led to a high number of deaths. In the case of the Armenian genocide, we see the development, for the first time, of death camps. During the inter-war years in Europe, we see the construction of camps to isolate 'undesirables' and 'asocials' (ethnic or political) from the rest of the population. This occurred after Europe's multinational empires had collapsed and when new nation states were attempting to build new societies based on new ideologies. The Soviet gulag was the exemplar for this kind of camp and may have been the model for the Nazi concentration camp system. There are no definitive figures for Soviet Russia, but archival evidence points to the development of a complex system of prisons, labour camps, labour colonies, and special settlements. As many as 18 million people passed through the hundreds of labour camps and colonies between 1930 and 1953, of which an estimated 1.6 million died in the camps, and possibly millions more after being released in poor health from the camp system. Another 800,000 people were executed in various purges between 1921 and 1953.

Researchers at the United States Holocaust Memorial Museum recently documented 42,500 ghettos and concentration camps built by the Nazis between 1933 and 1945, a figure far higher than previously thought. The Nazis built death camps from the end of 1941 (Chelmno, Belzec, Sobibor, Treblinka, Majdanek, and Auschwitz-Birkenau) but in Nazi ideology, ethnically undesirable inmates were never seen as a source of slave labour. They were used for labour, but the goal was not to preserve their lives for the war effort, but to work the inmates to death. They were not so much part of the war economy but lives to be 'wasted'. If the Spanish and British policies led to inadvertent deaths, the Nazis intended to starve the Jews and Slavs to death through precisely calculated starvation diets. More than 3 million Soviet POWs died in German camps, mostly from starvation and disease. It is estimated that over 1 million German POWs died in Soviet captivity, about one-third of all German POWs held by the Soviets.

After the Second World War, the use of camps continued in countries where the colonized were fighting for independence, such as Algeria, Malaya, and Kenya; as a means for dictatorships to isolate political opponents, such as Spain and Argentina; as well as in newly formed and often Communist states. China and North Korea have concentration camp systems that persist to this day, systems in which the camp is not only used as a means of 're-educating' individuals and reshaping society but has also become part and parcel of the (forced labour) economy. The camp, therefore, serves many purposes, but it tells us that the modern state is prepared to intern, as well as kill or let die, millions of its own people to strengthen or maintain its hold on power. If millions died in camps, however, millions were also killed by rifle and machine-gun fire or died of starvation in the killing fields (Ottoman, German, and Russian) of Europe.

## Genocide

Genocides have existed throughout history, and they invariably happen as a result of a process of dehumanizing that takes place *before* genocidal killing begins. Whether we are talking about American Indians, the Herero, Armenians, Jews, or Tutsis, the killers were conditioned to look upon people as 'lice', 'cockroaches', and 'vermin' that needed to be eradicated. Modern genocides, however, raise larger questions about the nature of the state, and the relationship of the state to its citizens. In the modern era, mass violence in the years leading up to the outbreak of the First World War was largely over religious/ethnic questions as states began to embrace 'national' identities and began to exclude those they now considered 'other' or enemies of the state. The trend continued after the First World War when there was the possibility of a massive ethnic reorganization, a redrawing of the map, that led to new national forces imposing their new national/ethnic identities onto the peoples of the borderland regions in question. The first of these occurred in the Ottoman Empire in the summer of 1915 with the decision made by the Committee of Union and Progress (CUP) to deport and then to exterminate the Armenian people. In 1929, Stalin began the collectivization of agricultural land that rapidly evolved into a class war against 'kulaks'. Hitler's reordering of central and eastern Europe was limited by his failure to defeat the Soviets in 1941. The Nazis had decided on a massive programme of colonization and resettlement of eastern Europe even before Operation Barbarossa, the invasion of the Soviet Union, in June 1941. This is known as *Generalplan Ost*, which foresaw the displacement of anywhere between 30 and 50 million people, many of whom were expected to die. That is, genocide was implicit in the plan. The brutal reality was that at least 10 million people were killed in the Nazi camp system between 1933 and 1945, a figure which encompasses the Holocaust.

The term 'genocide' was coined in 1944 by a Polish Jewish lawyer, Raphael Lemkin (1900–59), in a book documenting the Nazi policy of systematically destroying national and ethnic groups, including the mass murder of European Jews. He formed the word by combining *geno*, from the Greek word for race or tribe, with *cide*, from the Latin word for killing. Noting that the term denoted 'an old practice in its modern development', Lemkin defined genocide as 'a coordinated plan of different actions aiming at the destruction of essential foundations of the life of national groups, with the aim of annihilating the groups themselves'.

In 1948, in the shadow of the Holocaust and in no small part due to the efforts of Lemkin, the United Nations approved the Convention on the Prevention and Punishment of the Crime of Genocide. This convention establishes 'genocide' as an international crime, which signatory nations 'undertake to prevent and punish'. It defines genocide as: (a) killing members of the group; (b) causing serious bodily or mental harm to members of the group; (c) deliberately inflicting on the group conditions of life calculated to bring about its physical destruction in whole or in part; (d) imposing measures intended to prevent births within the group; (e) forcibly transferring children of the group to another group.

The United Nations definition was very much of its time, that is, influenced and modified as a result of Cold War politics. The Allies made sure that it precluded any accusations of genocide that might have been directed at them, such as the mass killings relating to aerial bombardment, while the Soviets made sure that the crimes notoriously associated with its regime, such as collectivization, mass deportations, or the Stalinist purges, were also excluded. Social and political groups were excluded from the definition. Moreover, not only is the United Nations definition vague, but the 'in part' qualification highlighted above makes it even more ambiguous. Since then, scholars have attempted to refine the definition—there are more than 22 in use—and to redefine categories of killing to include terms like ethnic cleansing, politicide, democide, gendercide, ethnocide, and genocidal massacre. Each of these terms, which differentiates between types of violent group action, can be used to describe a specific form of mass killing, but they are all part of the 'master-concept' that is genocide.

Related to the definition of genocide is the question of intent. While the United Nations definition assumes that genocide is premeditated and deliberate, some genocide scholars have opted for a more wide-ranging definition, arguing that indirect killing and destruction should also be taken into consideration. This is the case for much of the settler colonial world, where the destruction of native habitat and the spread of European diseases, as well as the direct killing of local inhabitants, led to the dramatic decline of indigenous populations. In this view, the argument goes, if the outcome looks like it is genocide then it is genocide.

Apart from the question of what makes genocide what it is, there is the question of what makes genocide possible. Zygmunt Bauman, a Polish-born sociologist and philosopher, argued that the Holocaust was a direct consequence of modernity and in particular the Enlightenment. He argued that totalitarianism was the result of rationalism taken to its extreme, so that the Holocaust was deeply rooted in modern, western civilization. Bauman also argued that several conditions had to be met for genocide to be committed. It had to be driven by a strong, technologically and bureaucratically efficient state; it had to be part of a rational process of elimination; and it had to have an ideological justification as well as a blueprint for creating a new world. Bauman also stressed that once mass political violence is unleashed, it develops its own dynamic and becomes all but unstoppable. For sociologist Michael Mann on the other hand, genocide occurs in the midst of 'geopolitical instability' and 'competing ideological projects'; it is more about ethnic rivals vying for power. Thus, in the former imperial powers, as well as in their colonial dominions, a form of national homogenization occurs as the democratic (or democratizing) state kills and displaces ethnically diverse populations. Both Bauman and Mann believe, however, that genocide is modern, and requires an ideological framework, such as race, or religion, or class, with a wide support base. It also, according to them, requires a technological capacity to kill on a large scale.

Many genocides in history, however, do not meet these criteria. The killing of around 600,000 to 800,000 Tutsis in Rwanda in the space of 100 days (around 75 per cent of the Tutsi population) did not require any sophisticated technology—machetes and starvation were the means used. It was genocide at an intimate, personal level, the kind of face-to-face killing that leaves us perplexed by the ease with which it was carried out. One can say the same for the men who belonged to the *Einsatzgruppen* and the Order Police Battalions on the eastern front during the Second World War. Those groups eliminated over 2 million people, largely by conventional means. Similarly, in Cambodia, it appears that most of the killing was done face to face, with machine guns, machine pistols, and rifles. That seems to contradict Baumann's technologically driven genocide with an ideological rationale. On the other hand, many pre-modern genocides were also framed in terms of religion or ethnicity. The term could apply, for example, to the killing of Cathars (a Christian sect considered heretic) in 12th-century France. What are we to call the destruction of indigenous peoples in the Caribbean at the beginning of the 16th century, if not genocide? It highlights just how difficult it is to determine exactly not only what genocide is but under what conditions it occurs.

## Explaining killing and mass atrocities in warfare

Of significance here is the ability of the individual to kill when called upon to do so by the community or the state. How are we to understand the willingness of people to kill on such a large scale? Much has been written by social scientists and social psychologists about why people, seemingly uncoerced, take part in killing, especially when it comes to mass murder and genocide. Perpetrator Studies, as it is known, is now a growing field, but it can largely be categorized under three theories: structural, intentional, and situational. Structural explanations emphasize the role of bureaucracies in organizing the killing. The individual killer assumes a subordinate role in this framework. In the case of the Holocaust, the destruction of the Jews became an administrative problem, a process which apparently neutralized moral concerns. Killing becomes part of a bureaucratic process and is thus impersonal. I think the problem with this approach is the assumption that the bureaucrat is completely distanced and that the decisions are impersonal, but we don't know if this is entirely the case; more work needs to be done on the bureaucratic mechanisms of killing.

Intentional/cultural accounts do the exact opposite and insist on the 'choice' of individuals in taking part in mass murder.

Perpetrators often do so uncoerced and with a certain degree of enthusiasm. But there is more to it than that. The philosopher, Thomas Nagel, puts it this way:

> What we do is also limited by the opportunities and choices with which we are faced, and these are largely determined by factors beyond our control. Someone who was an officer in a concentration camp might have led a quiet and harmless life if the Nazis had never come to power in Germany.

Nagel goes on to speculate that Germans under Nazi rule did no more than fail a test of civic courage. I imagine that most people would probably fail that test under the same circumstances, but then most of us will never find ourselves in a situation where we must make a choice between killing and not killing. What we want to try and understand is not only why people kill but also why a minority refuse to carry out the order to do so.

Situational explanations attempt to account for the murdering individual by considering how people react in certain environments. Central to this approach is conformity of behaviour. In that context, social scientists often point to classic experiments of Stanley Milgram in which the subjects absolve themselves of all responsibility by obeying authority, or of Philip Zimbardo, in which the subjects overwhelmingly conform to the behaviour of the group in which they find themselves. There is an ongoing debate about just how valid these experiments are in explaining the formation of a murderous mentality, but the 20th century is replete with examples. These are all valid approaches, but it is also worth looking at other understandings of massacre and atrocities in history. Massacres do not inevitably lead to genocide, but there can be no genocide without incremental massacres.

The first use of the term massacre in France in the 16th century came from the name for a butcher's knife, the *massacreur*. There is, nevertheless, a lack of consensus as to what constitutes a massacre. The pre-eminent scholar in the field, Jacques Sémelin, defines massacre as 'a form of action that is most often collective and aimed at destroying non-combatants'. However, this does not consider the blurred lines between combatant and non-combatant in many theatres of war, civilians who kill combatants, or the number of victims necessary to make up a 'massacre'. Let's broaden that definition then to include one group's intent to kill another group—generally unarmed and of any age or sex—for racial, religious, political, or cultural motives.

Common to massacre, as with all forms of mass killing, is a sense of superiority (racial, religious, cultural, or political) among the perpetrators over the victims. It is why massacres are often found in colonial or frontier settings. Atrocities often come from a position of weakness, that is, they are a response to the perpetrators' own fear of being attacked—violence as a defensive mechanism that had little to do with ideology or excessive aggression. The killing can come from below—soldiers or settlers seeking revenge for the death of their own—or it can be ordered from above, as a strategy to instil fear in civilians so that they think twice before resisting occupation. In some instances, massacres are deliberately carried out to force people to flee (think of the massacre of Palestinians carried out by Jewish forces during the 1947–8 war in Palestine).

Battlefield atrocities have also been a part of warfare since humans began killing one another in a concerted, relatively organized fashion several thousand years ago. No army in history has been wholly innocent of the charge. The use of massacre in the modern world is hardly a new development and is strikingly like the use of massacre by all states in the pre-modern era as a political and military tool to enforce obedience from rebellious lower orders. This was once considered entirely acceptable from a political and a military perspective, even if the excesses which the military were sometimes guilty of shocked elite sensibilities. In Europe, it was only in the 19th century that massacres of civilians by soldiers began to be hidden from public view, although they continued to occur in warfare throughout the 19th and 20th centuries, and in recent wars in the Middle East. Indeed, massacres are likely to occur wherever occupying troops interact with civilian populations.

In the modern era, ethnicity (and to a lesser extent religion) is a determining factor in whether one survives a conflict. This was certainly the case for the First and Second World Wars. Putting to one side for a moment the debates over German geopolitical ambitions, the First World War was also very much about nationalist and ethnic conflict in central and eastern Europe. The kinds of tensions that were unleashed among hugely diverse ethnic and religious populations with the collapse of the European empires (Russian, German, Austrian, and Ottoman) in the contested eastern European borderlands existed before the First World War, but they were contained by the European imperial states. In the aftermath of the war, however, the social and political instability in these regions spiralled into ongoing political violence. The historian Timothy Snyder suggests that if you draw a triangle from Estonia in the north of Europe to encompass Yugoslavia and Ukraine in the south—what he calls the 'bloodlands'—you were much more likely to suffer a violent death there than in any other region of the world, at least in the first half of the 20th century. Omer Bartov and Eric Weitz refer to these regions—extending from the Baltic to the Black Sea—as the 'shatterzone' or the European rimlands. Admittedly, not all the killing that took place was racially motivated—a good deal of it was carried out by the Soviets for ideological reasons—but much of it derived from pre-existing ethnic hatreds.

The Second World War, again putting to one side German and Japanese geopolitical ambitions, was driven in part by racial ideology. This was the case for the Nazis in Europe, particularly in eastern Europe, but it was also the case in the Pacific, where Europeans and other Asian forces fought the Japanese, who dehumanized their enemies, considered themselves superior, and who imposed a Greater Asia Co-Prosperity Sphere, which inflicted desolation on the Asian countries they occupied. The Japanese occupation and the mistreatment of civilians under their rule led to the deaths of around 6 million people, including Chinese, Koreans, Malaysians, Indonesians, Filipinos, and Indochinese, among others.

Allied troops often regarded the Japanese in the same way that Germans regarded Russians—as *Untermenschen* (subhumans). General Thomas Blamey, who commanded the Australian forces in New Guinea during the Second World War, told his troops that their foes were 'a cross between the human being and the ape, vermin, something primitive that had to be exterminated to preserve civilization'. Such sentiments were also widespread among Americans, furious at what they considered to be the treachery and cowardice of Pearl Harbor, such that boiling the flesh off enemy skulls to make souvenirs was not an uncommon practice. Allied soldiers in the Pacific 'collected' ears, bones, teeth, and skulls as souvenirs or trophies, a practice which, according to some soldiers' memoirs, was widespread. The Japanese in China did the same. Nothing comparable among combatants took place in Europe during the war, although German soldiers were very much in the habit of taking trophy photos of the humiliation of Jews and of killings and massacres.

Consider the photo in Figure 6, which shows Natalie Nickerson, 20, gazing at a skull—reportedly of a Japanese soldier—sent to her from New Guinea by her boyfriend serving in the Pacific. Is the skull illustrative of the kind of gruesome battlefield humour that men rely on to get through the horror of war, or does this signify a certain pride in their military success? We don't know who the Japanese soldier was, how the remains got into the hands of the navy lieutenant, or indeed what the young woman thought of the whole thing. Did the 'collector' have to boil the flesh off a decomposed head? Nor do we know what became of the skull or,

**6. Natalie Nickerson gazing at a skull of a Japanese soldier.**

indeed, of the young woman herself, or the man who sent it to her as a 'gift'. We only know what *Life Magazine*'s editors wrote about the photo, taken by Ralph Crane, when they featured it as a Picture of the Week in a May 1944 issue:

> When he said goodbye two years ago to Natalie Nickerson, 20, a war worker of Phoenix, Ariz., a big, handsome Navy lieutenant promised her a Jap. Last week Natalie received a human skull, autographed by her lieutenant and 13 friends, and inscribed: 'This is a good Jap—a dead one picked up on the New Guinea beach.' Natalie, surprised at the gift, named it Tojo. The armed forces [*Life* pointedly noted] disapprove strongly of this sort of thing.

In Europe, Germans, many imbued with the ideology of the master race, fought Slavs and Bolsheviks—and in the Nazi mindset Bolshevism was a Jewish ideology—in what was a war of racial annihilation. Casualty figures from the eastern front compared with other theatres of operation demonstrate the scale and the nature of the destruction. The total Allied losses, including both civilians and military personnel, in both the Pacific and European theatres, was around 1.5 million people. That's a lot of people but compare it to the German losses of around 10 million and the Soviet losses of around 27 million, the majority of them civilians. The number of people killed in France during the war represented about 1 per cent of the pre-war population. In Poland, anywhere between 16 and 20 per cent of the population was killed. There was not a family in Poland that was not directly touched by the war. In France and in the Netherlands, only one town in each country was razed by the SS in retreat. In Russia, by contrast, more than 3,000 villages were wiped from the map, and that is not counting Ukraine and other eastern European states. The suffering in eastern Europe was immense and compounded a pre-war history of Soviet political violence and famine.

It would be a mistake to think that the kinds of massacre and atrocity associated with the eastern front during the Second World War were in some way unusual. That kind of extreme violence is all too common in warfare. The photo in Figure 7 appeared in *Life Magazine* and was taken by a US Army photographer, Ronald L. Haeberle, during the My Lai massacre of 1968 in Vietnam. It shows mostly dead women and children on a road. The war reporter Seymour Hersh broke the story on the Associated Press wire service about one year after the massacre, and the newspapers soon followed. My Lai was the deadliest of several massacres committed by American troops that we know of. Many others may have gone undetected and unreported. Massacre studies often focus on the victims, but what of the killers? Private First Class Varnado Simpson was a black American soldier who took part in the My Lai Massacre when 347 Vietnamese civilians

**7. Photo of the My Lai massacre in March 1968 in Vietnam.**

were shot by C Platoon led by Lieutenant William L. Calley Jr. Some of the women were gang raped and killed, and their bodies mutilated. Simpson, who spoke openly about his behaviour in later years, was so overcome with guilt that he committed suicide in 1997.

Not all killers behave that way, or feel remorse, or are visibly marked by what they have done and what they have seen. Take, for example, a former Khmer Rouge prison guard, who was interviewed in his home while he bounced a baby on his knee. The man was responsible for the deaths of seven pregnant women and is accused of killing 2,000 people with a farm implement. And yet, on that day, in his house, he was a grandfather, a kindly man, seemingly no different from any other Khmer peasant. His victims, on the other hand, knew him as a killer. Reinhard Heydrich, the Nazi responsible for the coordination of the Holocaust, was, according to his biographer, Robert Gerwarth, 'an extremely sensitive violinist who displayed a tenderness and sentimentality that deeply impressed his audiences'. That might be true, but as recent research has shown, the SS and their police auxiliaries willingly participated in rituals of rape, sexual humiliation, and torture, often fuelled by alcohol, before, during, and after mass shootings in eastern Europe.

## Terror bombing

Atrocities against civilians were not only widespread, but they were also systematic during the 20th century. Take the Allied destruction during the Second World War of civilian cities, such as Dresden, Hamburg, Tokyo, Hiroshima, and Nagasaki. Cities have always been besieged and bombed but the invention of the aeroplane in the early 20th century allowed belligerent forces to bomb cities from a distance as never before. The first Hague peace conference in 1899 enshrined the principle that civilian cities could be attacked. From that time on, the air war techniques used by European armies were first perfected in the colonies, not only killing civilians but also destroying their homes, crops, animals, and livelihoods. The first bomb dropped from a plane was in Tripoli in 1911 when Italians bombed a Turkish encampment. The French followed suit in Morocco in 1911. After the First World War, the British in Iraq and on the Afghan north-west frontier in the 1920s, the Italians in Ethiopia, and the Germans in Spain during the Civil War all experimented with 'terror bombing', including the use of phosgene and mustard gas attacks. 'Terror bombing' is designed to break civilian morale, a goal that has never been achieved. In reality, it's designed to kill as many people as possible. 'Terror bombing' reached its peak during the Second World War, resulting in anywhere between 300,000 and 600,000 civilian casualties in Germany. Many Britons were in favour of the reprisal bombing of German cities. The goal was to raze completely all cities with a population of over 100,000 people. A similar policy was practised against Japan. Many Americans not only enthusiastically supported the bombing of Japanese cities, but some were in favour of the extermination of all Japanese. In the modern era, this kind of mass killing by airpower is no longer considered acceptable—although the annihilation of humanity was an ever-present possibility during the Cold War (and still is)—and has been replaced by the precision bombing of military targets through so-called smart bombs and drones.

There are two ways of understanding the mass killings that took place in the first half of the 20th century. The first is to compartmentalize each event, to examine them within a specific historical context (place and time), and to explain each event as the result of the development of a particular national-international history or a particular culture. The second is to examine mass murder as a European-wide event taking place simultaneously across a multinational landscape and with the support of many kinds of people. Viewed this way, the focus is on form over context. It is what genocide scholars often do when they discuss the theoretical implications of mass killing. Both approaches are valid and both approaches yield interesting insights.

## Terrorism

If the state has been responsible for the greatest number of deaths in the modern world, violence can also be used as a means by organized groups to achieve political, religious, or ideological ends through terrorism. All revolutionaries or terrorists who wish to subvert or violently overthrow the existing social order transform violence into a sacred if not a sublime device. Anarchists, Marxists, jihadists, and the western military have that in common. The revolutionary or freedom fighter willing to kill his or her opponents, the suicide bomber willing to kill and die for the cause, and the western world's readiness to use force to overthrow states (such as Afghanistan and Iraq) to bring about democratic reform all valorize violence as a necessary (and not necessarily 'evil') means to a just end. Radical political parties and organizations are willing to use violence to achieve their goals, often at the expense of innocent civilians. In fact, civilians often become a target in this struggle to create a new and better society.

So, what is terrorism? The term has evolved significantly over the past two centuries. Up until the 19th century, 'terror' had only ever been implemented by the state on individuals; think of the Terror during the French Revolution or spectacular public executions. That flipped when the terms 'terrorism' and 'terrorist' were used to describe Russian anarchists in the 1870s and 1880s bent on overthrowing the tsarist regime. It was clandestine, it was political, it was violent, and it was revolutionary; terror came from below, and not from above. In the 20th century, groups that most typified that kind of violence were the Algerian resistance movement, the Irish Republican Army, and the Palestine Liberation Organization (PLO), including the many offshoots that came out of these movements like the Red Army Faction in Germany, or the Red Brigades in Italy. The difference between 19th- and 20th- and 21st-century terrorists is that the former targeted political elites, while the latter target ordinary people. The PLO was involved in some spectacular terrorist attacks, such as the hijacking and detonation of four planes that were bound for New York City and London in 1970, and the Munich Massacre of 1972. Terrorism is both politics and theatre. Nevertheless, state-directed terror—think of Augusto Pinochet's Chile— continued and continues to exist wherever dictatorships and dictators rule by violence and intimidation.

The term terrorism has always had negative connotations and is often used by governments to delegitimize different kinds of political dissent, or any kind of radical attacks on government and capitalism. Militant vegans and anti-abortion crusaders, who sometimes use the term 'genocide' to describe industrial farming, and who raid industrial pig farms or abattoirs, have been dubbed 'terrorist' by certain sections of the conservative establishment. That's nonsense on both counts and highlights the kinds of misuse or overuse that terms of violence can encourage. The term 'terrorism' can be both an epithet and a category of analysis, but the old adage 'one man's freedom fighter is another man's terrorist' underlines how difficult it is to come to an objective definition of the term. Terrorists are called that by others, not themselves. Some argue, however, that it's possible to arrive at a definition of terrorism based upon accepted international laws and principles regarding what is and is not permissible in conventional wars. This can range from assassinations of public figures to random attacks on civilians (think of the bombings in Madrid in 2004, in London in 2005, the attacks in Mumbai in 2008, and in Paris in 2015). But there are problems with definitions, which now tend to exclude state-based actors. To paraphrase Noam Chomsky, it's hard to find a definition that excludes the terror *we* carry out against *them* and includes the terror that *they* carry out against *us*.

It is not unheard of for governments to use and indeed to exaggerate the threat of terrorism to push through laws that restrict individual freedoms. In Australia, for example, where billions of dollars have been spent on bolstering 'national security' and fighting the 'war on terror' since 2001, a total of 12 people have been killed in terror-related incidents (including the suspected terrorists). (This doesn't include 10 Australians killed on 11 September 2001, or the 88 Australians who died in the Bali Bombing of 2002.) However, during that same period, over 800 women and over 250 men were killed in domestic violence incidents, while only $700 million was committed to fighting that social problem. Similar figures exist in other industrialized countries. In Britain, 126 people were killed in terrorist-related incidents between 2000 and 2018, with £2.6 billion invested in 'national security' every year. Between 2000 and 2018, 1,870 people were killed in domestic violence related incidents in England and Wales. Another 400 people committed suicide because of domestic abuse. There is no doubt that national security agencies throughout the world have foiled terrorist plots, although it is impossible to say how many innocent lives may have been saved as a result. One can nevertheless ask, given the disparity in the numbers of deaths, whether the response to these two problems—terrorism and domestic violence—has been proportionate. It comes back to the question of why some forms of violence are considered worse than others, but also to why and how governments, the media, and the public prioritize some forms of violence over others.

Terrorist groups, like revolutionary organizations, adopt a 'good versus evil' mentality (as do the states that fight them) that excludes those who do not belong to the group. While 19th-century terrorist groups relied on knives, guns, and dynamite to implement attacks that were dubbed 'propaganda of the deed', terrorist attacks in the 21st century can be far deadlier. Terrorism, after all, is meant to terrify. The Bali Bombing of 2002 killed 202 people and wounded hundreds more; the Madrid train bombing of 2004 killed 191 and wounded over 1,800; the London underground train bombing of 2005 killed 52 and injured over 700; the Mumbai terror attacks of November 2008 killed more than 174 people and wounded more than 300. In January 2015, Boko Haram attacked the town of Baga in Nigeria and killed up to 2,000 people. That same year, attacks in Paris killed 130 people and wounded 494. The media coverage of these last two events in the western press disproportionately focused on the killings in Paris, influencing how the west 'feels' for the victims of violence.

As we can see from these examples, terrorism can be, for want of a better term, a cost-effective way of fighting a more powerful enemy, usually a state. It doesn't take much to kill hundreds of people—a simple explosive, a gun, as we saw with the mosque shooting in Christchurch, New Zealand, on 15 March 2019, that resulted in 51 killed and 40 injured, or a truck, as we saw with the so-called 'lone wolf' attack in Nice in 2016 in which a troubled young man drove a truck into crowds celebrating Bastille Day, killing 86 and wounding hundreds more. However, successful terrorist organizations are more than just lone wolf attacks. They require a high degree of technological and communication skills, not to mention communities of support. That's why they are often made up of well-educated militants, who come from relatively affluent backgrounds. They often develop hierarchical, professionalized, militarized organizations with elaborate structures that resemble modern bureaucracies. They also often have propaganda units in charge of recruiting and justifying their brutal acts of killing. Religion may play a role in some terrorist organizations—Al-Qaeda, for example—although there is debate about the extent to which individuals in those organizations are motivated by religious or political beliefs to commit acts of violence. This 'new terrorism', one that has religious inflections, makes it very distinct from past acts of terrorism. In terrorist organizations that declare themselves Islamic, martyrdom is high on the agenda. This is a relatively new approach to terror, even if the theological underpinnings of violent jihad and martyrdom are to be found in interpretations of the Qur'ān.

Modern terrorist acts have a number of features in common: they are usually spectacularly violent (a plane hijacking, an assassination of a public figure, the beheading of aid workers, or a car or suicide bombing); they are generally aimed at civilians; and they are designed to strike fear into large sections of the civilian population, as well as possibly to destabilize governments. The reasons terrorist attacks occur, and what motivates terrorists, are as varied as the individuals belonging to the militant political groups behind them. As with every form of violence, context is everything. Political scientist David Rapoport has pointed to 'four waves' of modern terrorism: the 'Anarchist Wave', which went from the 1890s through to 1914; the 'Anti-Colonial Wave' from the 1920s through to the 1960s; the 'New Left Wave' from the 1960s through to the 1990s; and the 'Religious Wave', which began with the 1979 Iran hostage crisis and persists to this day. It's during this wave that a shift took place from targeting powerful elites to aiming for mass casualties.

I would add that a fifth wave appears to be emerging—right-wing extremism. A report by the United Nation's Security Council's Counterterrorism Committee points to the dramatic rise in right-wing terrorism globally in the five years prior to 2020. Most of those attacks are carried out in western countries: think of Christchurch in New Zealand (March 2019), El Paso in the United States (August 2019), and Halle (October 2019) and Hanau (February 2020) in Germany. According to the University of Maryland's Global Terrorism Database, there were 310 terrorist attacks resulting in 316 deaths in the United States from 2015 to 2019. Most originated with right-wing extremists. This is now a global problem.

## The decline of killing in warfare?

The ability to kill in warfare increased dramatically between the first use of the Gatling gun in 1862 during the American Civil War and the testing of thermonuclear weapons in 1952. During that 90-year period, the world experienced gas deployed on the battlefield during the First World War—and in the death camps during the Second World War—not to mention the subsequent development of chemical and biological weapons, as well as 'carpet bombing' and the strafing of civilians by planes. There was the invention of tanks, flamethrowers, and napalm (the extermination of the enemy by fire by other means), torpedoes and submarines, and more recently drones, all capable of inflicting severe loss of life. It is often thought that chemical weapons were only used during the First World War, but in fact incendiary bombs were also chemical weapons that caused far more deaths during the Second than in the First World War— around 350,000 people suffocated to death in firestorms during the Second World War, compared to 90,000 killed by incendiary bombs during the First World War—not to mention their deployment in conflicts in the Middle East in the 21st century. What is interesting is that the belligerent powers did not use newly developed nerve gas during the Second World War despite having had access to it. It was possibly an early example of mutual deterrence. The Washington Conference of 1921 prohibited the use of gas in warfare, but during the inter-war period there were those, such as Captain B. H. Liddell Hart, who went on to become a military historian, who argued that gas was a more 'humane' weapon than bullets or bombs, also implying that it would also be a cost-effective method of putting down rebellions in the colonies.

Some figures from the two world wars help give an idea of the scale of killing. The First World War resulted in 9.7 million battle casualties. The war on the western front was largely a monstrous artillery duel in which millions of shells were lobbed over the trenches; German artillery alone fired over 222 million rounds. Sixty per cent of the fatalities from that war resulted from bombs or shells of one kind or another, because of which a new term was invented—'shell shock'. This is the beginning of the psychologizing of the consequences of modern warfare that eventually came to be recognized as Post Traumatic Stress Disorder.

For the 20th century, both the time it took to get medical care after injury and the improvement in medical care itself considerably reduced mortality rates. For American combat injuries in the First World War, the average time from injury to treatment was 12–15 hours, with a mortality rate of 8.5 per cent. This time dropped to 6–12 hours in the Second World War, and mortality dropped to 5.8 per cent. During the Korean War, often cited as an era of major advances in trauma care, treatment occurred between 2 and 4 hours of injury, with a dramatically improved mortality rate of 2.4 per cent. In Vietnam, treatment could occur as early as 1 to 2 hours after injury with a mortality rate levelling at 2.6 per cent. By the time we come to the wars in the Middle East in the first decades of the 21st century, troops could be transported to a combat support hospital in 30–90 minutes.

At the same time, the number of battle deaths per year, worldwide, has dropped since the end of the Second World War, with just a few spikes largely explained by the Korean War (1950–3), the Vietnam War from the mid-1960s to the mid-1970s, and the strife in the Balkans and among former Soviet republics in the 1990s. The pattern of the past century is that the deaths of non-combatants due to war has risen very dramatically. In the First World War, perhaps only 10 per cent of the 10 million who died were civilians. The number of non-combatant deaths jumped to as much as 50 per cent of the 50 million-plus lives lost in the Second World War, and the civilian toll has kept on rising ever since. Perhaps the worst, but hardly the only, terrible example of this trend can be seen in the war in the Democratic Republic of Congo (1996–2003), in which over 90 per cent of the several million dead were non-combatants.

As for the number of wars fought since the end of the Second World War, the *Human Security Report,* looking at the period 1946–2008, shows a steady rise to over 50 wars per year in the early 1990s (225 armed conflicts between 1946 and 2001, of which 115 took place in the 12-year period between 1989 and 2001). The rest of the 1990s saw a drop in conflicts of about 40 per cent—to a great extent driven by the ending of the Balkan and post-Soviet wars—and then a pattern of rising armed conflict once again after 9/11. The number of wars is down by over one-third since the peak in the 1990s, but ongoing conflicts today are still more than double the totals seen in the years from the end of the Second World War until the mid-1950s and are equal to the numbers of wars going on during the Vietnam era. The number of civil wars appears to have increased since 1945 as wars between states have become less common. It is hard to describe this, as do scholars like Steven Pinker, as a world in which war is on the wane. When the state no longer completely controls the mechanisms of violence the results can be calamitous.

And the reasons why individuals take part in acts of collective violence on behalf of the state, or in the case of terrorists, against the state? One could argue that generalizations about why people kill do not enlighten us very much. They might do so out of opportunism, careerism, or racism, or there might be questions of honour and a perverse sense of duty involved, or they might do so out of religious or ideological conviction, or out of a confluence of these factors. Based on what we have witnessed in history over the centuries, all humans are capable of committing acts of violence, and perhaps even atrocities, in the right circumstances, if the cultural, social, religious, and political context is ripe. And we are not simply talking about young men committing acts of violence but both genders and across all ages. Women are as capable of committing atrocities as men, as we can see with female concentration camp guards. If they don't do so on such a large scale as men, I would argue it is because violence is often tied to perverted notions of masculinity. It nevertheless begs the question, have we really changed all that much over the centuries, or is the capacity to kill a constant that is hidden within us until it emerges in the right circumstances?

# Chapter 7
# The changing nature of violence

There is necessarily much that has not been covered in a short introduction of this nature, including systemic structural and institutional violence. Social factors such as class, poverty, gender, and race pose persistent problems and can lead to both physical and emotional acts of violence. Some historians have argued that there is no empirical evidence demonstrating that the modern economy, the modern state, modern manners, or modern science have had any long-term impact on humanity's predisposition to violence. On the contrary, they argue that the scale of collective brutality dramatically increases with the rise of modern social organizations while the character of interpersonal violence remains essentially the same. That said, when nation building is successful, rates of violence tend to be low. But when nation building fails, rates of violence tend to be high. Similarly, there is an argument that as the state increased its hold over people and some forms of violence (such as public executions) declined, other forms of violence, such as domestic violence, became far less public. There is some indication that gendered and interpersonal violence is on the rise in some countries around the world. At the same time, according to a United Nations report from 2016, more countries experienced violent conflict than at any point in the last 30 years.

As we have seen, the state can both diminish violence while at the same time being responsible for some of the worst crimes committed in the 20th century, from concentration camps and gulags to the elimination of political and ethnic 'enemies'. There is no one ideology or indeed a particular form of state that is solely responsible for mass killings in the 20th century. Democratic states are just as likely to respond in violent ways to perceived threats to their authority and just as likely to commit ethnic cleansing and genocide as totalitarian states. This was especially the case for the 18th and 19th centuries, although less so for the 20th and 21st centuries (so far). Nevertheless, ideology played a significant role in war objectives during the Second World War (Communism, Fascism, Nazism), and consequently had a tremendous impact on the levels of killing.

If violence can be driven by official state policy, it can also be carried out by violent communities or groups of sub-state actors over which the state or the authorities have little or no control. This was often the case on the colonial frontier, but it is also sometimes the case in zones of war. The eastern front during the Second World War is a case in point, but so too was the Partition of India in 1947. During one of the largest migrations in human history, millions of Muslims trekked to West and East Pakistan (now Bangladesh) while millions of Hindus and Sikhs headed in the opposite direction. Many hundreds of thousands never made it.

As for interpersonal violence, it is impossible to measure with any degree of accuracy those forms of violence that are termed private—especially domestic violence, child abuse, sexual assault, and rape—largely because they are either not reported or significantly under-reported. Whether we experience violence in the world today, or whether we consider violence to have increased or decreased over time, is very much dependent on race, class, and gender. If one is white, middle class, and living in an affluent society, it is possible to never encounter an act of violence during one's lifetime. That's not the case in many parts of the world, however.

I want to end this book by looking at different kinds of violence that have emerged in the modern world, acts and institutions which were once not considered violent, but which now are. Incarceration is an example of an institution that is rarely seen as violence. It is often seen as a more humane form of punishment than say, corporal punishment, but that is not always the case. There are about 9–10 million people in prison around the world, half of whom are in the United States, China, and Russia, where people are held in such poor conditions that their mental and physical well-being suffers. Physical and sexual violence tends to be high in prisons. In several western countries—Australia, Britain, France, and the United States—minorities are often over-represented in both numbers of incarcerated and in the numbers killed by the police. The highest rates of indigenous incarceration of any country in the world are in Australia.

Modern-day human trafficking, although it is usually not for life and is often associated with contemporary migration movements, is also considered to be a particularly pernicious form of violence. According to the latest statistics by the International Labour Organization and the Walk Free Foundation, there are more than 40 million people in the world today who are 'forced to work, through fraud or threat of violence, for no pay beyond subsistence'. This is what the ILO calls the 'underside of globalization'. Around 30 per cent are trafficked for sex while 70 per cent are in situations of forced labour. Modern estimates for slavery and human trafficking range widely (depending on the methods used to estimate the number and the definition of slavery being used), but the number could be as high as 100 million men, women, and children; we simply don't know. Most of the trafficking occurs in Asia, particularly across the Greater Mekong region of Cambodia, China, Laos, Myanmar, Thailand, and Vietnam. There is no doubt that slavery is flourishing—there are more slaves in the world today than existed during the whole of the Atlantic slave trade—and it has evolved over time to cater for rising consumer demand in the world for cheap goods and cheap sex.

The sexualization of violence has become a prominent feature of video gaming and virtual spaces. In addition, the web has become a site in which abuse is rife, not only against women; but when it does involve women, it generally involves threats of violence, rape, and other physical attacks. Public humiliation and shaming on the internet, where people can hide behind their anonymity, has become routine, but so too has violence against women. The pillory and public shaming, it would seem, have not really left us; they have just taken on new forms. Men are also harassed online, but by far the biggest target is women. The abuse experienced by women is often sexist or misogynistic in nature; online threats of violence against women are often sexualized and often make specific references to women's bodies. According to one study carried out by Amnesty International, black women were disproportionately targeted by online abuse and were 84 per cent more likely than white women to be mentioned in abusive or problematic tweets. Women of colour were also more likely to be mentioned in such tweets than white women. We don't know the scale of the abuse because Twitter won't provide any data. Why should this matter? Because things like 'revenge porn', cyber harassment, and trolling can have real-life effects on people, inducing psychological disturbances such as anxiety, depression, and PTSD, and real-life consequences including drug and alcohol abuse, self-harm, and suicide.

Can we say the same for hyper-violent video games or what has been dubbed 'torture porn' in feature films? In visual media one can see gratuitous, highly sexualized, extreme forms of violence that have increased in tempo and cruelty over the years. That is part of the contradiction of human nature. We can at the same time be both repulsed by real violence and titillated by imaginary violence. But it also goes to the interplay between culture on the one hand and the brain, biology, and behaviour on the other. Neurohistory might show the way here. It's built on the premise that emotions can have an impact on the ways in which neurochemicals react. The very fact that the things that we do, and see, and experience can have an impact on our moods—that is, that culture can have an impact on our psychology (and possibly vice versa)—is at the core of this approach and is meant to encourage us to ask why and how this can happen.

We can extend our historical examination of violence to what humans have done and are doing to the environment and the animal world. Environmental disasters and the mass extinction of animals brought about by humans have been referred to as slow violence, which is incremental rather than spectacular. This is a kind of structural and systemic violence that often forms the background to more spectacular eruptions of violence such as warfare, but there is also a connection between what has been called ecocide and genocide in many parts of the world. More animals are now killed for human consumption, not to mention the depletion of the world's oceans, than at any previous time in human history. As our environmental awareness grows, the industrial farming of animals and the killing of wildlife for consumption is also being seen as violence. Reliable statistics on the annual slaughter of farm animals around the world are difficult to obtain, but in 2004 the United Nations' Food and Agriculture Organization (FAO) estimated that hundreds of millions of animals (horses, sheep, cows and calves, goats, turkeys, rabbits), and billions of ducks and chickens are killed every year in factory-like animal-processing centres.

Whatever forms of violence we may be confronted with, social and political change can only come about through increased and accurate statistical data, which can feed into broader social awareness. Social awareness can lead to movements that result in changes in attitudes, and that consequently can lead to a less violent world. Put another way, how we decide to interact with violence, what we choose to remember and what we choose to forget, what we choose to focus on as a pressing social and political issue and what we choose to ignore, is a dynamic and constantly shifting cultural, political, and social phenomenon. What remains constant in our human history, however, is the enduring presence of the traces of acts of violence at the individual, community, and state level, whether they are officially sanctioned or not. These are permanent reminders of the impact of violent acts whether, as Primo Levi so eloquently put it, they are privately engraved on people's hearts or recalled in public forums. The haunting shadows that have been cast by violence indelibly remain with us.

# References

## Chapter 1: Violence past and present

Warren Brown, *Violence in Medieval Europe* (Harlow: Longman Pearson, 2011).

D. R. Carrier and M. H. Morgan, 'Protective Buttressing of the Hominin Face', *Biological Reviews*, 90 (2015), 330–46.

Francisca Loetz, *A New Approach to the History of Violence: 'Sexual Assault' and 'Sexual Abuse' in Europe, 1500–1850* (Leiden: Brill, 2015).

Hisashi Nakao, Kohei Tamura, Yui Arimatsu, Tomomi Nakagawa, Naoko Matsumoto, and Takehiko Matsugi, 'Violence in the Prehistoric Period of Japan: The Spatio-temporal Pattern of Skeletal Evidence for Violence in the Jomon Period', *Biology Letters*, 1 March 2016, <https://doi.org/10.1098/rsbl.2016.0028>.

Pieter Spierenburg, 'Violence: Reflections about a Word', in Sophie Body-Gendrot and Pieter Spierenburg (eds), *Violence in Europe: Historical and Contemporary Perspectives* (New York: Springer, 2008), 13–25.

## Chapter 2: Intimate and gendered violence

Goerge K. Behlmer, 'Deadly Motherhood: Infanticide and Medical Opinion in Mid-Victorian England', *Journal of the History of Medicine and Allied Sciences*, 344 (October 1979), 403–27.

Joanna Bourke, *Rape: A History from the 1860s to the Present* (London: Virago, 2007).

Joanna Bourke, 'The Rise and Rise of Sexual Violence', in Philip
  Dwyer and Mark Micale (eds), *The Darker Angels of our Nature:
  Refuting the Pinker Theory of History and Violence* (London:
  Bloomsbury Academic, 2021).

Shani D'Cruze, *Crimes of Outrage: Sex, Violence and Victorian
  Working Women* (DeKalb, Ill.: Northern Illinois University
  Press, 1998).

Lisa Hajjar, 'Religion, State Power, and Domestic Violence in Muslim
  Societies: A Framework for Comparative Analysis', *Law & Social
  Inquiry*, 29/1 (Winter 2004), 1–38.

Michelle T. King, *Between Birth and Death: Female Infanticide in
  Nineteenth-Century China* (Stanford, Calif.: Stanford University
  Press, 2014).

J. Robert Lilly, *Taken by Force: Rape and American GIs in Europe
  During World War II* (Basingstoke: Palgrave Macmillan, 2007).

Amy Dellinger Page, 'Gateway to Reform? Policy Implications of
  Police Officers' Attitudes Towards Rape', *American Journal of
  Criminal Justice*, 33/1 (May 2008), 44–58.

## Chapter 3: Interpersonal violence

Mark Cooney, 'The Decline of Elite Homicide', *Criminology*, 35/3
  (1997), 381–407.

Arne Jansson, *From Swords to Sorrow: Homicide and Suicide in Early
  Modern Stockholm* (Stockholm: Almqvist & Wiksell, 1998).

Randolph Roth, *American Homicide* (Cambridge, Mass.: Belknap
  Press of Harvard University Press, 2009).

James Sharpe, *A Fiery & Furious People: A History of Violence in
  England* (London: Random House, 2016).

Gerd Schwerhoff, 'Criminalized Violence and the Process of
  Civilisation: A Reappraisal', *Crime, Histoire & Sociétés/Crime,
  History & Societies*, 6/2 (2002), 103–26.

Robert Shoemaker, 'The Decline of Public Insult in London,
  1660–1800', *Past and Present*, 69/1 (2000), 97–131.

Richard Slotkin, *Regeneration through Violence: The Mythology of the
  American Frontier 1600–1860* (Middletown, Conn.: Wesleyan
  University Press, 1973).

Pieter Spierenburg, *A History of Murder: Personal Violence in Europe
  from the Middle Ages to the Present* (Cambridge: Polity, 2008).

## Chapter 4: The sacred and the secular

Marcus A. Doel, *Geographies of Violence: Killing Space, Killing Time* (Los Angeles: SAGE, 2017).

V. A. C. Gatrell, *The Hanging Tree: Execution and the English People, 1770–1868* (Oxford: Oxford University Press, 1996).

Lela Graybill, *The Visual Culture of Violence after the French Revolution* (Farnham: Ashgate, 2016).

Mark Juergensmeyer, *God at War: A Meditation on Religion and Warfare* (New York: Oxford University Press, 2020).

Randall McGowen, '"Making Examples" and the Crisis of Punishment in Mid-Eighteenth-Century England', in David Lemmings (ed.), *The British and their Laws in the Eighteenth Century* (London: Boydell and Brewer, 2005), 182–205.

## Chapter 5: Collective and communal violence

Micah Alpaugh, *Non-Violence and the French Revolution: Political Demonstrations in Paris, 1787–1795* (Cambridge: Cambridge University Press, 2015).

William Beik, 'The Violence of the French Crowd from Charivari to Revolution', *Past & Present*, 197 (2008), 75–110.

Gema Kloppe-Santamaría, 'Lynching and the Politics of State Formation in Post-Revolutionary Puebla (1930s–50s)', *Journal of Latin American Studies*, 51/3 (2019), 499–521.

Charles Tilly, 'Collective Violence in European Perspective', in Ted Robert Gurr (ed.), *Violence in America: Protest, Rebellion, Reform*, 2 vols (Newbury Park, Calif.: SAGE, 1989), ii. 62–100.

## Chapter 6: Violence and the state

Noam Chomsky, 'Terrorism, American Style', *World Policy Journal*, 24/1 (1 March 2007), 44–5.

Mark Cooney, 'From Warre to Tyranny: Lethal Conflict and the State', *American Sociological Review*, 62 (1997), 316–38.

Robert Gerwarth, *Hitler's Hangman: The Life of Heydrich* (New Haven: Yale University Press, 2012).

Jonas Kreienbaum, 'Deadly Learning? Concentration Camps in Colonial Wars Around 1900', in Volker Barth and Roland Cvetkovski (eds), *Imperial Co-operation and Transfer, 1870–1930:*

*Empires and Encounters* (London: Bloomsbury Academic, 2015), 219–36.

B. H. Liddell Hart, 'Gas in Warfare, More Humane than Shells', *Daily Telegraph*, 15 June 1926.

Benjamin Madley, 'Patterns of Frontier Genocide 1803–1910: The Aboriginal Tasmanians, the Yuki of California, and the Herero of Namibia', *Journal of Genocide Research*, 6/2 (2004), 167–92.

Michael Mann, *The Dark Side of Democracy: Explaining Ethnic Cleansing* (Cambridge: Cambridge University Press, 2005).

M. M. Manring et al., 'Treatment of War Wounds: A Historical Review', *Clinical Orthopaedics and Related Research*, 467/8 (2009), 2168–91.

Thomas Nagel, 'Moral Luck', in George Sher (ed.), *Moral Philosophy: Selected Readings* (Fort Worth: Harcourt Brace College Publishers, 1996), 441–52.

Amanda Nettelbeck, 'Flogging as Judicial Violence: The Colonial Rationale of Corporal Punishment', in Philip Dwyer and Amanda Nettelbeck (eds), *Violence, Colonialism and Empire in the Modern World* (Cham: Palgrave Macmillan, 2017), 111–30.

Richard N. Price, 'The Psychology of Colonial Violence', in Philip Dwyer and Amanda Nettelbeck (eds), *Violence, Colonialism and Empire in the Modern World* (Cham: Palgrave Macmillan, 2017), 25–52.

Jacques Sémelin, *Purify and Destroy: The Political Uses of Massacre and Genocide*, translated by Cynthia Schoch (New York: Columbia University Press, 2007).

Patrick Wolfe, 'Settler Colonialism and the Elimination of the Native', *Journal of Genocide Research*, 8/4 (2006), 387–409.

# Further reading

Works on the history of violence have grown in recent years, reflecting a more focused interest in the subject. The four-volume *Cambridge World History of Violence* (Cambridge: Cambridge University Press, 2020), edited by Philip Dwyer and Joy Damousi, is a good entry into the field. Each chapter contains further reading suggestions. Volume iv is dedicated to the modern world. Dwyer's 'Violence and its Histories: Meanings, Methods, Problems', *History & Theory*, 56/4 (2017), 5–20, gives an overview of some of the problems associated with writing about violence in history. It can be read in conjunction with Peter Imbusch, 'The Concept of Violence', in Wilhelm Heitmeyer and John Hagan (eds), *International Handbook of Violence Research*, 2 vols (Dordrecht: Kluwer Academic, 2003), i. 13–39. The two volumes contain an array of chapters on different approaches and themes. An excellent sociological overview of violence is Siniša Malešević, *The Rise of Organised Brutality: A Historical Sociology of Violence* (Cambridge: Cambridge University Press, 2017). A very good summary of the debates around prehistoric warfare and violence is Andrea Dolfini, Rachel J. Crellin, Christian Horn, and Marion Uckelmann, 'Interdisciplinary Approaches to Prehistoric Warfare and Violence: Past, Present, and Future', in A. Dolfini et al. (eds), *Prehistoric Warfare and Violence* (Berlin: Springer, 2018), 1–18. For the debates about just how violent the past was, see the collection of essays edited by Philip Dwyer and Mark Micale, *The Darker Angels of our Nature: Refuting the Pinker Theory of History and Violence* (London: Bloomsbury Academic, 2021), which also contains a detailed bibliography of recent works on violence.

*The Routledge Handbook of Gender and Violence*, edited by Nancy
Lombard (London: Routledge, 2018), offers a comprehensive
introduction to the topic, as does *The Oxford Handbook of Gender,
Sex, and Crime*, edited by Rosemary Gartner and Bill McCarthy
(Oxford: Oxford University Press, 2014). Histories of rape are often
confined to Europe. Other than Bourke see Georges Vigarello, *A
History of Rape: Sexual Violence in France from the 16th to the
20th Century*, trans. Jean Birrell (Malden, Pa: Polity Press, 2001).
For sexual violence against children the Victorian era is particu-
larly rich. The best overview is Louise A. Jackson, *Child Sexual
Abuse in Victorian England* (London: Routledge, 2000). For the
United States see Stephen Robertson, *Crimes against Children:
Sexual Violence and Legal Culture in New York City, 1880–1960*
(Chapel Hill, NC: The University of North Carolina Press, 2005).
On infanticide see Mark Jackson (ed.), *Infanticide: Historical
Perspectives on Child Murder and Concealment, 1550–2000*
(Aldershot: Ashgate, 2002). Other than male-on-male rape, rape
in warfare is now a well-researched field. See Dagmar Herzog (ed.),
*Brutality and Desire: War and Sexuality in Europe's Twentieth
Century* (Basingstoke: Palgrave Macmillan, 2011);
Edward B. Westermann, *Drunk on Genocide: Alcohol and Mass
Murder in Nazi Germany* (Ithaca, NY: Cornell University Press,
2021); Yuki Tanaka, *Japan's Comfort Women: Sexual Slavery and
Prostitution During World War II and the US Occupation*
(London: Routledge, 2002); and Dara Kay Cohen, *Rape during
Civil War* (Ithaca, NY: Cornell University Press, 2016).

Apart from Spierenburg and Roth cited in the References, an overview
on the debates and approaches to homicide can be found in Philip
Dwyer, 'Violent Death', in Peter N. Stearns (ed.), *The Routledge
History of Death Since 1800* (New York: Routledge, 2020), 63–76.
More detailed reading lists can be found in the chapters by
Spierenburg in vols iii and iv of the *Cambridge World History of
Violence*. Again, the literature on homicide is often country
specific. For the quantitative dimension of the history of homicide
in Europe, Manuel Eisner, 'Long-Term Historical Trends in Violent
Crime', *Crime and Justice*, 30 (2003), 83–142. On suicide, see
Marzio Barbagli, *Farewell to the World: A History of Suicide*
(Cambridge: Polity, 2015).

On the history of torture and the disappeared during the Cold War,
especially in Argentina, see James P. Brennan, *Argentina's Missing
Bones: Revisiting the History of the Dirty War* (Berkeley;

University of California Press, 2018); and Federico Finchelstein, *The Ideological Origins of the Dirty War: Fascism, Populism, and Dictatorship in Twentieth Century Argentina* (Oxford: Oxford University Press, 2014). On torture more generally see J. Jeremy Wisnewski, *Understanding Torture* (Edinburgh: Edinburgh University Press, 2010); and, although focused on America, W. Fitzhugh Brundage, *Civilizing Torture: An American Tradition* (Cambridge, Mass.: Harvard University Press, 2018). On the history of crime and punishment in England see James Sharpe, *A Fiery & Furious People: A History of Violence in England* (London: Random House, 2016). On the history of capital punishment in Europe, see Richard Evans, *Rituals of Retribution: Capital Punishment in Germany, 1600–1987* (Oxford: Oxford University Press, 1996); and Pieter Spierenburg, *The Spectacle of Suffering: Executions and the Evolution of Repression. From a Preindustrial Metropolis to the European Experience* (Cambridge: Cambridge University Press, 2008). On religion and violence, the collection of essays edited by Mark Juergensmeyer, Margo Kitts, and Michael Jerryson (eds), *The Oxford Handbook of Religion and Violence* (Oxford: Oxford University Press, 2016), is a good starting point. On the relation between extremist violence and religion see Mark Juergensmeyer, *Terror in the Mind of God: The Global Rise of Religious Violence* (Berkeley: University of California Press, 2003). On immolation, see K. M. Fierke, *Political Self-Sacrifice: Agency, Body and Emotion in International Relations* (Cambridge: Cambridge University Press, 2013).

Charles Tilly's work on *Collective Violence* (Cambridge: Cambridge University Press, 2003) is a classic. An overview of revolution can be had in Jack A. Goldstone, *Revolutions: A Very Short Introduction* (Oxford: Oxford University Press, 2114). On the pogrom in Russia see Elissa Bempora, *Legacy of Blood: Jews, Pogroms, and Ritual Murder in the Lands of the Soviets* (New York: Oxford University Press, 2019). A comprehensive review of the literature on lynching in America can be found in Michael J. Pfeifer, 'At the Hands of Parties Unknown? The State of the Field of Lynching Scholarship', *Journal of American History*, 101/3 (2014), 831–46. On black rebellion in America see Peter Levy, *The Great Uprising: Race Riots in Urban America during the 1960s* (Cambridge: Cambridge University Press, 2018); and Elizabeth Hinton, *America on Fire: The Untold History of Police Violence and Black Rebellion since the 1960s* (New York: Liveright,

2021). On the putative decline of violence in warfare, see Joshua S. Goldstein, *Winning the War on War: The Decline of Armed Conflict Worldwide* (New York: Dutton, 2011). On the bombing of civilians in war there is A. C. Grayling, *Among the Dead Cities: Is the Targeting of Civilians in War Ever Justified?* (London: Bloomsbury, 2006); and more generally, Alexander B. Downes, *Targeting Civilians in War* (Ithaca, NY: Cornell University Press, 2012).

On the concentration camp, Dan Stone, *Concentration Camps: A Short History* (Oxford: Oxford University Press, 2017). A detailed analysis of the Russian camp system is in Anne Applebaum, *Gulag: A History* (New York: Doubleday, 2003). A recent, controversial revision is Golfo Alexopoulos, *Illness and Inhumanity in Stalin's Gulag* (New Haven: Yale University Press, 2017). The Nazi camp system is thoroughly treated by Nikolaus Wachsmann, *KL: A History of the Nazi Concentration Camps* (New York: Farrar, Straus & Giroux, 2016). The literature on genocide is vast but good overviews can be had in Eric D. Weitz, *A Century of Genocide: Utopias of Race and Nation* (Princeton: Princeton University Press, 2003); and Benjamin A. Valentino, *Final Solutions: Mass Killing and Genocide in the Twentieth Century* (Ithaca, NY: Cornell University Press, 2004). A wonderful short overview of corporal punishment is Guy Geltner, *Flogging Others: Corporal Punishment and Cultural Identity from Antiquity to the Present* (Amsterdam: Amsterdam University Press, 2014). The literature on colonialism and violence is extensive although it usually focuses on particular regions or empires. Some notable examples are Adam Hochschild, *King Leopold's Ghost: A Story of Greed, Terror and Heroism in Colonial Africa* (Boston: Houghton Mifflin, 1999); Mike Davis, *Late Victorian Holocausts: El Niño Famines and the Making of the Third World* (London: Verso, 2002); J. P. Daughton, *In the Forest of No Joy: The Congo–Ocean Railroad and the Tragedy of French Colonialism* (New York: W. W. Norton, 2021); and Caroline Elkins, *Legacy of Violence: A History of the British Empire* (New York: Knopf Doubleday, 2022). Comprehensive surveys on terrorism include David C. Rapoport (ed.), *Terrorism: Critical Concepts in Political Science*, 4 vols (New York: Routledge, 2006); Bruce Hoffman's *Inside Terrorism* (New York: Columbia University Press, 2006); and Carola Dietze and Claudia Verhoeven (eds), *The Oxford Handbook of the History of Terrorism* (Oxford: Oxford University Press, 2014).

On incarceration in America, see Elizabeth Hinton, *From the War on Poverty to the War on Crime: The Making of Mass Incarceration in America* (Cambridge, Mass.: Harvard University Press, 2016). On the relationship between ecocide and genocide, Emmanuel Kreike, *Scorched Earth: Environmental Warfare as a Crime against Humanity and Nature* (Princeton: Princeton University Press, 2021). On modern slavery, Kevin Bales, *Disposable People: New Slavery in the Global Economy* (Berkeley: University of California Press, 1999).

# Index

For the benefit of digital users, indexed terms that span two pages (e.g., 52–53) may, on occasion, appear on only one of those pages.

Violence

# CHAOS
## A Very Short Introduction
Leonard Smith

Our growing understanding of Chaos Theory is having fascinating applications in the real world - from technology to global warming, politics, human behaviour, and even gambling on the stock market. Leonard Smith shows that we all have an intuitive understanding of chaotic systems. He uses accessible maths and physics (replacing complex equations with simple examples like pendulums, railway lines, and tossing coins) to explain the theory, and points to numerous examples in philosophy and literature (Edgar Allen Poe, Chang-Tzu, Arthur Conan Doyle) that illuminate the problems. The beauty of fractal patterns and their relation to chaos, as well as the history of chaos, and its uses in the real world and implications for the philosophy of science are all discussed in this *Very Short Introduction*.

'... Chaos ... will give you the clearest (but not too painful idea) of the maths involved ... There's a lot packed into this little book, and for such a technical exploration it's surprisingly readable and enjoyable - I really wanted to keep turning the pages. Smith also has some excellent words of wisdom about common misunderstandings of chaos theory ...'

popularscience.co.uk

www.oup.com/vsi

# SEXUALITY
## A Very Short Introduction
Veronique Mottier

What shapes our sexuality? Is it a product of our genes, or of society, culture, and politics? How have concepts of sexuality and sexual norms changed over time? How have feminist theories, religion, and HIV/AIDS affected our attitudes to sex? Focusing on the social, political, and psychological aspects of sexuality, this *Very Short Introduction* examines these questions and many more, exploring what shapes our sexuality, and how our attitudes to sex have in turn shaped the wider world. Revealing how our assumptions about what is 'normal' in sexuality have, in reality, varied widely across time and place, this book tackles the major topics and controversies that still confront us when issues of sex and sexuality are discussed: from sex education, HIV/AIDS, and eugenics, to religious doctrine, gay rights, and feminism.

www.oup.com/vsi